F DYING

HOW CHEATING DEATH KICKED MY ASS INTO LOVING, LEARNING, AND LIVING MY BEST LIFE

Dan Clark

The author of this book does not dispense medical advice or prescribe the use of any or the techniques as a form of treatment for physical, emotional, or medical problems without the advice of a physician either directly or indirectly. The intent of the author is only to offer information of a general nature to help you in your quest for emotional and spiritual well-being. In the event that you use any of the information in this book for yourself, the author and publisher assume no responsibility for your actions.

FIRST EDITION

DanNitroClark.net
FDying.com

Library of Congress Cataloging-in-Publication Data
Names: Clark, Dan, author.
Title: F Dying: how cheating death kicked my ass into loving, learning and living my best life / Dan Clark
Description: 1st Edition | Los Angeles, California: Gladiator Events, LLC 2017
Identifiers: LCCN 2017914121
Subjects: Self-Actualization
SELF-HELP / General | SELF-HELP / Personal Growth / Success

ISBN 978-0-9993517-1-0 Hardcover
ISBN 978-0-9993517-0-3 Paperback
ISBN 978-0-9993517-2-7 Ebook

Sports taught me about life.

Almost dying taught me how to live.

TO MY FAMILY

Contents

INTRODUCTION.......9
Chapter 1: A Moment of Clarity.......17
Chapter 2: Why Me?.......33
Chapter 3: One Step at a Time.......41
Chapter 4: There Is Beauty Everywhere.......49
Chapter 5: I Can't Explain the Tears.......59
Chapter 6: A Simple Practice That Saved Me.......65
Chapter 7: Lift People Up.......75
Chapter 8: Love Yourself First.......87
Chapter 9: I'm Glad I Had a Heart Attack.......97
Chapter 10: What Kind of Life do You Want to Live?...103
Chapter 11: Adults Need Recess Too.......113
Chapter 12: Spandex Rules.......123
Chapter 13: Use Me, God.......129
Chapter 14: Play that Funky Music.......139
Chapter 15: Your Secret Weapon.......145
Chapter 16: What You Do Is Not Who You Are.......153

Chapter 17: Do What Scares You 161
Chapter 18: The Time to be Brave is Now 173
Chapter 19: The Secret About Love 181
Chapter 20: The Thief of Joy 189
Chapter 21: It's Not Always About You 193
Chapter 22: The Value of Valuing Others 203
Chapter 23: Forgiveness 207
Chapter 24: Love and Relationships....................................215
Chapter 25: Broken, Yet More Beautiful 225
Chapter 26: All We Can Do Is *Everything* We Can Do...231
Chapter 27: In the End It's Simple.......................................237
Share 243
APPENDIX: INSTRUCTIONS 245
WITH GRATITUDE 261

INTRODUCTION

I want to die.

I never thought I'd say those words.

I've always thought of myself as a positive, "glass half full" type of guy. I had what most people would consider a good life. I was fit, healthy, had a big house, drove a German car.

Then on Wednesday, December 18, 2013, my world changed: I had a heart attack.

In an instant, I went from a world where everything seemed possible to a world where I knew nothing was for certain.

As a life-long athlete, former professional football player, and American Gladiator, I'd always put a tremendous value on health, fitness, and what I could do with my body. The heart attack wasn't only a derailment of my life—it shattered the entire definition of who I was.

I was weak. Fragile. Broken.

I believed life would never be good for me again, and I thought if I couldn't live life on my terms, then there wasn't any point in going on. The day after the heart attack, lying in my hospital bed, miserable out of my mind, I uttered those four words.

I want to die.

During the course of our lives, many of us will have something tragic happen suddenly. It could be a cancer diagnosis, a sick child, a divorce, a business deal gone badly, or something as heartbreaking as a dream that goes unfulfilled. It's difficult to find strength in the face of adversity.

Yet, we've all hit hard times, we've all struggled, we've all fallen down. The question is: What do we do when these things happen?

For every setback there is a chance to make a comeback and rise again. The human spirit has an amazing capacity to persevere. I've seen it happen time and time again. But for me, it was about more than just coming back; it was about coming back transformed. Coming back as a better man.

The following pages are my journey from "I want to die" to some of the happiest and most profound times of my life. I'll share with you what helped and what didn't. Where I succeeded and, perhaps more importantly, where I failed.

Looking back on my life before the heart attack, I can't believe how much time I wasted on things that didn't matter with people who did matter. Most of my happiness came from what I accomplished. I believed the key to happiness was to achieve more, do more, acquire more. I was shocked to learn that my accomplishments didn't create peace of mind and my possessions only brought temporary satisfaction.

I chased gratification but rarely felt grateful or fulfilled. I was constantly stressed, struggling to find balance and hardly ever felt at peace. I thought about what I wanted while rarely appreciating what I had. If I did allow myself to feel good it was only for a brief moment, because I was afraid that if I felt happy for too long I'd lose my edge.

No matter what I did, I couldn't figure out a way to create *sustained* happiness. I assumed this was just the way life was, even though deep down I longed for a better way to live.

Then I got the gift of *not dying.*

Facing your mortality shines a light on what you love in life, your reason to live, and how you want to live.

I realized one of the scariest things in life is to do what we actually want to do. We put off following the dreams deep in our hearts and get lost in the busyness of life. We run around checking things off our "to-do" list but rarely feel like we've spent enough time on what's important. We work harder than we ever have, yet it feels like we never have enough. And, at the end of the day we collapse in our beds exhausted, wondering where all the time went.

We live in a time where we have more than we've ever had yet we feel less and less happy. We feel isolated, empty and alone. We crave authenticity, community and connection.

Most of us have two lives. The life we live and the *unlived life* within us. This book is my attempt to share what I believe makes a life worth living.

I first shared what I learned from the experience with my friends. They told me my story had a remarkable effect on their lives, and how it not only improved their perspective on life, but also made them happier.

I spoke about my experience more and more, not only with my friends but many others. I spoke about gratitude, cultivating happiness, pursuing the dreams deep in your heart, and how time isn't guaranteed. I also spoke at different public venues and conferences. Nearly everyone I spoke to felt inspired, motivated, moved, and told me how much what I shared meant to them.

Even with all of this positive feedback, it was still hard to decide to write this book.

Truth be told, I was afraid what people might think. I'm a former professional athlete, I'm known for being a tough guy; it's fine to write about health and fitness, kicking life's ass, taking no prisoners. But this stuff?

I then shared my fears with my uncle Steven Farmer, who also happens to be a doctor of psychology and author of ten books. He told me, "You have to share this. It's more important than 'Here's how to get ripped abs' or anything else you could write. This story will change lives."

That's when I realized sometimes the hardest things to do are the most important—and that's how we ended up here.

This book is about what I've learned in the past four years since the heart attack. It's meant to be a companion, a guide, and a spark that ignites a fire in you, to live better, be happier and appreciate every moment of your life.

As you turn the page, I want you to remember a time when you felt anything was possible.

That
Time
Is
NOW.

Oh yeah, one more thing…

F Dying.

Here's to really living.

Chapter 1: A Moment of Clarity

Why can't I breathe?

I try to pull in a breath but only gasp.

What the hell is going on? Here I am, one of the more fit people in my cardioflex class, and I'm falling behind. I've been a professional athlete and now make my living from fitness. This doesn't make sense.

But I feel so short of breath I have to stop. I hunch over, hands on my knees to try and catch my breath. I look around as everyone else continues on.

Ten seconds pass. Fifteen seconds. Twenty.

I suck in a deep breath and push myself back into the workout. After about a minute, I'm gasping again. It feels like I'm running up a hill even though I'm barely moving.

It's a strange sensation. My mind rifles through the reasons. Again, I take a glance at the other participants in class—they are cruising along.

Something's not right.

Pressure hits my chest followed by a sharp stabbing pain there.

It feels like I'm climbing Mount Everest and breathing thinner air with each step.

Step, inhale.

Step, exhale.

I drop to a knee to catch my breath. No one seems to notice.

I sit longer this time, assessing what I feel. Twenty seconds. Thirty seconds. A minute. My mind shuffles through a handful of possibilities: pulled muscle, something I ate, a cold or virus, didn't get enough sleep, a supplement I took, heartburn...that one seems to stick.

I get back to my feet and start to work out again. I've trained myself to push through pain. I've always felt that the difference between me and a lot of other people is that I've been able to push through pain that would make others quit.

That's my competitive advantage, that and being willing to do the work to get what I wanted when others weren't.

But this is something different. I can intuitively tell something isn't right. Yet, I can't wrap my mind around what.

Looking back it's odd, but I didn't consider the idea that it could be a heart attack. I've trained my entire life to be healthy, fit and strong. I eat really well. I take all the right supplements. I believed a heart attack could happen to anyone but me.

It just didn't occur to me then.

The more I push forward and exercise, the more I feel the stabbing pain in my heart.

I dig my fingers into my chest to try and relieve the pain.

I struggle to breathe. Still can't seem to get full breaths into my lungs.

I know something is wrong. I stop training and walk over and sit on the couch in the back of the gym. I catalogue the symptoms in my mind.

Shortness of breath.

Chest pain.

I rub my forehead. My hand comes away soaking wet. In fact, I'm dripping wet. I'm not working out hard enough to sweat like that—*it's a cold sweat.*

That's when I look down at my left arm and notice I've been subconsciously shaking it to alleviate the pain radiating down it.

I go over the symptoms again.

Shortness of breath.

Chest pain.

Cold sweat.

Numbness down my left arm.

Panic starts to set in. I know these are the classic symptoms of a heart attack, but I still don't believe it could be one. There has to be some other explanation.

I'm too healthy.

Too young.

Too strong.

My friend Ben walks by. I call him over and ask him to grab my cell phone in the cubby 10 feet away. I don't tell him that I'm afraid to move. Fearful that if I do, the hand grabbing my heart will squeeze and I'll die.

Ben hands me my cell phone. I secretly text my girlfriend. I don't want to draw attention to myself. I don't want to seem weak.

> *911. Call me.*

I wait. Seconds tick by. Ben sees the look on my face and asks if I'm okay. I start to go over the symptoms with him.

Chest pain. Shortness of breath. Numbness down the left arm. Cold sweat.

We both know these are the symptoms of heart attack, but neither of us mention it because heart attacks don't happen to people as healthy as we are. When someone has a heart attack, they clutch their chest, collapse to the ground and writhe in pain.

I've seen it on the movies. I've read about it in the papers.

This wasn't that.

Ben thinks maybe I pulled a muscle in my back or shoulder. I shake my head, no. Tell him it's something different, that I know my body pretty well but can't explain what this is.

I still don't want to admit that it could be a heart attack.

Ben suggests I go to Urgent Care to get it checked out. I nod in agreement and ask him if he can drive. It's always been hard for me to ask for help. It's hard even now. Ben agrees and we quietly walk to the car. I don't want any attention on me. I don't want anyone to be alarmed. I still believe whatever this is, it will pass.

I slide into the car and adjust the seat so I can lie back. The pain starts to intensify. It now feels like someone is stepping on my chest. My left elbow is bent and my forearm rests on my stomach as if my arm is in a sling. My right hand massages my chest, trying to release some of the pressure.

The pain starts to radiate up my neck into my jaw as a wave of nausea passes over me. I'm still afraid to move, still fearing that whatever is grabbing my chest will squeeze and I'll die.

It's rush hour in L.A., the worst time to get anywhere. The seconds drip by. The urgent care is only three miles away but it takes us 20 minutes to get there. I hurry inside, moving as quickly as I can in my current state.

A young woman, about 25, is behind the desk. I approach her hunched over in my workout clothes, covered in sweat. I grumble, "Chest pain... left arm..."

She hands me a stack of paperwork and tells me to fill it out.

I roar back at her, "I'm having chest pain! Shortness of breath!"

She recoils. A doctor rushes out from the back. He hurries me into a room where he starts applying

EKG electrodes across my body as I lie back on the examining table.

The EKG whirs and clicks to life. Moments later the results spit out.

The doctor looks at me and says, “Mr. Clark, you’re having a heart attack.”

The words hang in the air. I look at him in disbelief. This can’t be happening to me. They’ve got the diagnosis wrong. I’m too young. I’m too healthy. A heart attack could happen to anyone BUT me.

I take a deep breath and try to digest the doctor’s words. They just rattle in my brain and get stuck there like a ball bouncing off of a wall.

Mr. Clark, you’re having a heart attack.

In an instant I go from a world where everything makes sense to a world where I know nothing for certain. I sit with my head slumped. My body slack. My mouth is dry. For a moment, I panic and forget to breathe.

I feel waves of emotion roll deep within me. I feel vulnerable. I feel weak.

I've spent my whole life trying to be strong. Whenever weakness would creep through the gates and rise to the surface, I'd grab it by the throat and choke the very life out of it. Now, here I am.

I'm having a heart attack.

I am weak, fragile and pathetic.

I am *broken.*

The room is covered in a thick haze. I look at the doctor. He's a blur in white. I see his lips moving. It takes a long moment to absorb and understand what he is saying.

"Mr. Clark? Mr. Clark, are you okay?"

I try to speak but I cannot.

"Mr. Clark, we need to call an ambulance and get you to the hospital immediately."

It takes everything I have to focus on the doctor.

"No ambulance," I mumble. "My buddy Ben can drive me to the hospital."

The doctor cuts his eyes at me and shakes his head, no. "I think it's better if we call an ambulance."

I'm still piecing everything together and trying to digest what's happening to me. I stammer and stutter. "I just let my insurance policy lapse at the beginning of December so I could get a new plan in January. I don't want to pay $5000 for a 15-minute ambulance ride when my friend Ben can take me. "

His voice is strong and determined. "Mr. Clark, I have to strongly advise against your friend taking you to the hospital."

"Why?"

"Because, if you die on the way to the hospital, it shouldn't be up to your friend to revive you."

It hits me. This is real. It's happening. I'm having a heart attack and I could... *die.*

This is the moment when I let go of everything and surrender to what was happening to me.

To the sound of the sirens.

To the paramedics entering and wheeling me away.

To having a heart attack.

To dying.

It's a weird thing to surrender control and let go. I hadn't realized until this moment how much I felt in control of every aspect of my life. Life is all about control. We control what we say, what we do, what we feel. We try and control everything.

I quickly realize that now it isn't up to me. I had to give up complete control and allow the paramedics and the doctors to tend to my failing body. I had to accept the reality that nothing I could do in that moment would make a difference.

When I give up control I find peacefulness in the surrender. It is a deeply satisfying, personal peace. As strange as it sounds, I am on the verge of death, and yet I'm feeling more peaceful than I have in a long time.

It takes four men to lift me into the ambulance. Strapped to the gurney, oxygen mask over my mouth, I bounce around in the back of the ambulance as we rush to the hospital. The ride becomes a cacophony of sounds with the blaring sirens and rattling of loose equipment. I hear the voices of the paramedics, each speaking in urgent, short bursts.

I get lost in the chaos and the noise until one thought rises over the fervor.

Let go. Surrender.

The paramedics shuttle me in through the ambulance entrance to the emergency room. I get the sensation that I am floating above my body watching the scene unfold far below me. I am in a great golden light and I experience myself as a transparent, radiant energy.

I can see all eyes on me as I pass by the waiting room lobby.

They steal quick glances.

I've been in the waiting room before when the paramedics have brought a person in on a gurney. I've always thought that person must be in really bad shape. They had to be. They brought them in an ambulance.

This time—I am that person.

I watch as I'm wheeled into a room. A host of nurses and doctors move around me. They work in a clear and concerted effort: sticking electrodes on me, poking me with needles, clipping things to my fingers, taking my blood pressure, performing an ultrasound.

The cardiologist starts to pepper me with questions. In that instant, I come back into my body.

"How long have you had the chest pain?" he asks.

It takes a second to orientate and answer.

"Since about 5 p.m."

He looks at his watch. "It's 7:45 now," he states. "So you have had the pain for almost three hours?"

I nod, yes. Instinctively, I know this isn't good.

"What were you doing at the time you first felt the pain?"

"I was working out in the gym. Nothing strenuous. Just doing cardio."

The questions keep coming at rapid pace.

Where is the pain mainly? What other symptoms did you have? Have you taken any drugs? Cocaine? Viagra? Do you have a family history of heart disease?

I answer the questions as quickly as the cardiologist asks them. While we talk, people are shoving the results of the tests in front of him.

I'm not sure how much time passes before the cardiologist looks at me and confirms that I am having a heart attack. He doesn't know how bad the damage is. Tells me he wants to get me to the operating room immediately to have surgery.

My girlfriend stands at the side of my bed. I can see the tears welling in her eyes.

The doctor continues, "Time is of the essence. Each second your heart doesn't get blood it damages the heart and the heart starts to die. Once you damage your heart tissue, it can't be replaced or fixed."

I look at the doctor. I need to know. "Am I going to die?"

He adjusts his glasses, chews on this for a second and says, "I don't think so. But I need to get you to surgery right away to see what's going on."

I don't think so?

Not the answer I want to hear. I feel myself tense up. I remind myself to let go and surrender again.

Nothing I can do will make a difference as to whether or not I will survive, or how much heart damage I have.

As soon as I surrender, and I mean completely surrender, I feel the incredible sense of peace return.

As they hustle me off to the operating room, I feel no fear. I am good with whatever happens. I realize that tomorrow will come and go no matter what happens to me.

I'm not saying goodbye. I am surrendering to an outcome I can't control.

Before the heart attack I'd always seen surrendering as a sign of weakness or defeat.

Now, I know it is a paradox. Sometimes we need to surrender to win.

When I truly surrendered, there was a peace that passed all my understanding.

My last thought as I entered surgery was to let go and surrender.

Chapter 2: Why Me?

I woke up in my hospital room. I'd been dealing with this new shocking reality for a few days now. My eyes scanned the austere room cloaked in shadows, across the hospital bed, the monitor displaying my vitals, the partial remains of my dinner, the IV stuck in my arm.

This wasn't somewhere I ever expected to find myself.

To say I was depressed would have been too pretty a description. I felt like everything I valued and worked for in life had been taken away from me.

As a kid, having endured my older brother dying in my arms when he was 12 and I was ten, I had empty spaces that loomed large inside me that sports filled. Sports were the first way I knew how to feel good about myself. It was the one area people complimented me on, from Pop Warner football, to high school ball to college football through the NFL to the *American Gladiators*, martial arts, and as a CrossFit competitor.

Being an athlete wasn't just something I did—it was my identity. The heart attack wasn't only a derailment of my life—it stole the entire definition of who I was.

When I was younger and had a setback, it was easy to bounce back with youthful optimism—because I knew not only did I have time, but there had to be a place in the world for me.

Now, the best times in life suddenly seemed so distant and unreachable. It was as if time had tapped me on the shoulder and in an instant life had passed me by.

I wondered if life would ever be good for me again.

I began to feel sorry for myself and started asking, "Why me?"

I'd done everything right. I exercised like a beast. I ate all the right foods. I took all the right supplements. My entire life was dedicated to health and fitness.

Of all people, I was not supposed to be the one who had a heart attack.

I felt an overwhelming assault of emotion surge through me. I felt weak and pathetic. I fought to push back the emotions and the tears. I wouldn't cry for myself. I wouldn't allow that to happen. I refused to be that pitiful grown man in the hospital crying and feeling sorry for himself.

But then something cracked, some fissure opened behind the hard façade. A rogue bud of moisture escaped, and spilled down my cheek. But just as quickly I wiped away the tear. Then I remembered...

Let go. Surrender.

The tears came in little waves until they became deep sobs. I buried my hands in my face and wept openly.

I was tired. Tired like I've never been before. My body hurt and ached. I was miserable, out of my mind. And I couldn't stop crying and feeling sorry for myself.

Why me? Why me? Why did this happen to me?

I was done with it. I was exhausted. I didn't care if my life was over. I began to wonder, *Why am I alive?*

A thought floated to the surface of my consciousness. In moments of desperation we will receive answers. We only need to listen.

I was alive to *feel.*

It's what every atom of our body is built for.

Without emotion, without love, without sorrow, life is just a clock ticking off the seconds until death.

I told myself it was okay to be sad. It was okay to weep. There is beauty in the fragility. To feel is to be human. Tears flowed.

Tears of sorrow.

Tears of regret.

Tears of loss.

I cried until I had no more tears. Then in the calm a new thought came to me.

Instead of thinking *Why me?* I started to think, *What could I be?*

The simple shift in thinking saved me. I kept repeating the question.

What could I be? What could I be? What could I be?

Once I focused my mind in the right direction, a light shone on me and the possibilities came thundering in.

I could be the guy who still stood tall after he had his identity stripped from him.

I could be a visible example of how great life can still be after a heart attack.

I could take a setback and turn it into a gift of inspiration for others.

I could be the change-maker. I could show people how to still hope, still dream after suffering a life-changing event.

As these thoughts swirled in my head, I started to see the hopes and dreams and possibilities that were still before me.

A light flooded into my brain. I had an acute realization. Through all of this, one thought became clear:

A broken heart doesn't mean a broken man.

That epiphany led me to another thought.

I have always been more than my body.

My body was simply an external manifestation of my spirit. My spirit was what helped me shine and overcome obstacles in the past.

My spirit was what helped me survive and flourish after watching my older brother die.

My spirit was what helped me find happiness again after my father died from an overdose.

My spirit was what helped me pick up the pieces and find love again after my divorce.

My spirit was what helped me keep my family together and help my son thrive after he suffered a life-threatening illness.

My spirit gave me the will and volition to go from a fat kid who was always picked last to playing in the NFL.

My spirit was what helped me accomplish everything and anything I'd done in my life.

My body was simply the armor, the shell that carried my spirit.

My heart might be broken, my physical abilities might be compromised, but inside I was still the same person. Inside of me there was still a light that burns bright.

This light was my spirit, and as long as I have a heartbeat I vowed to shine and burn bright or destroy myself trying. There was no middle ground.

In my hospital bed, in the darkness, with a world outside that would continue whether I lived or died, I set out to burn bright.

This vow became my anchor, the one true thing, as I faced what my life would be after a heart attack.

Chapter 3: One Step at a Time

Standing at the top of the stairs I felt a vulnerability that I cannot describe. It was my first day home from the hospital. My goal for the entire day was to walk down the stairs from my bedroom to the refrigerator and not die.

I wasn't ready to start. It hurt to move. I felt like I'd been hit by a truck. I was still having chest pain. I was afraid the simple journey down the steps would kill me.

The doctor warned me about doing too much too soon. He cautioned against stairs, lifting anything heavy, and pretty much doing anything. My heart was fragile and anything I did could cause another heart attack, he told me.

I reminded myself this is what the comeback trail looks like. There is no mile marker, no welcome mat, just my deep-rooted belief that for every setback there is a chance to come back and rise.

My mind flickered to my old goals: playing in the NFL, winning an Oscar, owning a multimillion dollar home, making the *New York Times* bestseller list, winning the CrossFit Games.

I realized that all of my goals had always been about external achievements that showed the world my worth. Never was one of my goals to be a *better man*. I felt a stab of regret. I had just assumed that being a better man would naturally happen as I pursued and achieved these goals.

I looked back down the stairs, to my entire goal for the first day. I knew I needed to start before I felt ready. There would never be a perfect time to begin. In order to get started, I just needed to start.

I thought back on my life... I don't believe there was ever a time I started any endeavor when I felt 100% ready. I sucked in a deep breath and gave myself a pep talk.

You got this.

You can do this.

Broken heart doesn't mean broken man.

It all felt like bullshit. I was still not ready to begin. I stared in dread at the stairs. It was only 22 steps, but it felt miles long. I sucked in another stiff breath. Took my first step. Stopped. Did a quick inventory.

Chest pain? No.

Shortness of breath? No.

I took the next step, stopped and asked the same questions.

Chest pain? No.

Shortness of breath? No.

It continued like this for each and every one of the 22 steps. Once I hit the bottom of the stairs, I exhaled, let go a little and made my way to the kitchen. There, I fell back into a chair and caught my breath.

The sun filtered through the window across my face and its warmth filled me. I wondered how I could have ever taken it for granted. I reveled in the beauty and the simplicity of the moment. I wanted to truly and deeply feel it.

The gratitude.

The appreciation.

Today my accomplishment is probably the smallest thing I've ever done in my life and yet, I felt good. I felt like I'd won a prize. I was happy. Here is the best part. I did win something. I accomplished my goal for the entire day. I made it downstairs to the refrigerator and lived.

I thought about how hard we make it to feel good about ourselves in life. We set out and create a list of nearly insurmountable goals and only allow ourselves to feel good when we accomplish them. Often, when we do the satisfaction is short lived because we are off trying to achieve the next thing.

We've become human *doings* instead of human *beings.*

My second day home, my goal for the entire day was to walk outside and touch my mailbox and not die.

The third day, the goal for the entire day was to walk to my neighbor's house and touch his front door and not die.

The fourth day I challenged myself to walk a few hundred yards to the corner, touch the stop sign and not die.

Each day, with the single-minded focus of an athlete, I pushed myself to go a little further—to extend my reach beyond my grasp. And each day I wrestled with the very real possibility that what I was doing might kill me. Yet, each day I moved forward.

It was thunderously clear to me that courage isn't the absence of fear—it's taking action even when you are afraid.

This thought buoyed me and helped me along the way.

After a few weeks, I got my cardiologist's okay to ride a stationary bike with no resistance. In my garage in the gray of an overcast day, I was barely pedaling on my stationary bike but to me it felt like I was riding in the Tour de France.

Every time I reached my new goal, no matter how small and simple it was, I allowed myself to feel good. Since I am half Japanese, I had made it a point when I was younger to study Asian philosophy. I remember a quote by the philosopher Confucius:

> *The man who moves mountains begins by carrying away small stones.*

Confucius could have added—with each small stone a man carries away he should feel happiness. And...the road to happiness is paved with small victories.

I continued to take steps forward every day, to carry away small stones, until 15 months after my heart attack I stood, drenched in sweat on a podium after winning a CrossFit competition.

I smile as I write this because, in all honesty, in the beginning I didn't think I'd survive. The odds were against me.

Last year 326,200 people experienced out-of-the-hospital cardiac arrests in the United States. Of those treated by emergency medical services, a scant 10.6 percent survived.

I'm filled with gratitude and appreciation.

I look back on the past 15 months and think of the things that helped me and saved me.

It was acting with courage even when I was afraid.

It was starting before I was ready.

It was celebrating the small, daily victories along the way.

It was learning to *happily achieve* instead of achieving to be *happy.*

Think about all the times we rush from one goal to another to cross another "to-do" off our list without ever allowing ourselves to feel good about our achievements and accomplishments.

We all get caught in the spinning wheel of success without ever letting ourselves feel positive about accomplishing anything. We fall into the "I'll be happy when..." syndrome. I'll be happy when I get a new job. I'll be happy when I find the perfect partner. I'll be happy when I finally buy a home. We continually delay our happiness until we accomplish a goal or reach a milestone.

Imagine this. Imagine living a life where you set small and manageable goals and allow yourself to actually feel good each day when you accomplish them. You celebrate you each and every day.

There is beauty in the simplicity.

There is happiness here.

Chapter 4: There Is Beauty Everywhere

The days are long but the years seem to go by quicker and quicker. Time is passing. When you face death you immediately take an inventory of what is most important. You instantly become aware of what really matters. Things that seemed so important a moment ago suddenly appear inconsequential.

Those were my thoughts as I sat on a bluff overlooking the ocean with the spring breeze brushing gently against my face. Blue skies, vastness stretched before me, unknown and beautiful.

I'd been here before, but had never appreciated the beauty. The beauty is not lost on me now.

I thought about how often the smaller moments like this tend to slip by us and go unnoticed. I riffled through my backpack, took out my notebook and wrote:

> You beat death by choosing how you are going to live with the time you have left.
>
> I choose to be happy.
>
> I choose to shine a light on the small moments.
>
> I choose to remember.

I took a deep breath in. I felt the stirring of dreams and happiness in my gut. I vowed each day that I'm conscious, I'll make the decisions to shine a light on these small moments. To not let them slip by. To trust and know that recognizing these small moments is the key to cultivating happiness.

In life too often we wait for the big moments to allow ourselves to feel good. The promotion. The big win. The finishing of a project. The birth of a child. Buying that first home. Getting married. These are all glorious moments and should be celebrated. But the juice of life and happiness is found in celebrating the small, everyday moments.

With that, I started writing furiously, creating a list of small moments of happiness, small moments of human truth.

Feeling wind on my face

Playing in the rain

Cherry blossoms

My son happy

Sounds of laughter

Every baby in the world

Puppies

A good cup of coffee in the morning

Kindness

Fireworks, especially unexpected ones

Piggyback rides

Hummingbirds

A rainbow

Sunsets

The smell of rain

My feet on the sand

Staying in bed on a Saturday

Feeling of fresh, clean sheets

When you find the perfect pillow

A nap on any afternoon

My favorite meal

My dogs

Finding out at the register something's on sale

Randomly running into a good friend

Walking in nature

That place in meditation where everything seems in sweet and simple order

A falling star

Sound of the waves crashing on the shore

Dinner with friends and no one is on their cell phone

There is Beauty Everywhere

Winning anything

No line at airport security

Getting upgraded for free

Window seat on an airplane

Giving a friend advice that actually helps

Helping someone accomplish something

Seeing anyone shine bright

When your favorite food is also healthy

When they announced bacon was okay to eat

Bright, shining smiles of my nieces and nephews

When your favorite song happens to play on the radio

When a fireplace is the only light in the room

Eating with your fingers

Taking your shirt off and not giving a shit

Getting on the freeway and there is no traffic

Discovering there is an app for just what you need

An unexpected thank you

Dance breaks

Hitting all the green lights

Turning the TV on and your favorite movie is on

Dental floss picks

When anyone quits smoking

Christmas lights

Finding a picture of yourself that you like

When you don't get a ticket after being pulled over

A good night's sleep

Finding peace in solitude

Finding money in the laundry

Witnessing an act of kindness

Opening the door for someone and they appreciate it

Finding an up-close parking spot

A checker in the grocery store opening a new line

When a person lets you go in front of them at the store

Taking your shoes off and walking barefoot

Watching someone you love sleeping peacefully

Going to sleep at night knowing your family is safe

I stopped writing, put down my pen and went over the list. Each one of these delectable, little happenings filled my heart with joy.

I am happy. I am fulfilled.

I now understand there are no ordinary moments.

Recent studies show that the *frequency* of your positive experiences is a much better forecaster of your happiness than the *magnitude* of your positive experiences. We all think of big experiences—winning an Oscar, buying a fancy sports car, going on a date with a movie star—when we think of what would make us happy.

But studies show that how good your experiences are doesn't matter nearly as much as the number of good experiences you have.

I'm convinced if you want to cultivate happiness and appreciate life more, then you should start today by creating a list and making a vow to shine a light on the smaller moments in life, the ones that in the past might have slipped by unnoticed or unappreciated.

The goal, if there is one, is to take a deep breath and fully feel these little moments of human truth and let the happiness in.

This practice is deceptively simple in its power.

When you are grateful for everything you have, including each moment, when you focus on simple things in life that make you smile, when you focus on beauty and love—your pain flies away and happiness beats a path to your door.

Do this consistently. You will be awed at the magic that occurs.

Chapter 5: I Can't Explain the Tears

I can't explain the tears.

I'm standing in the kitchen, all 6 feet, 2 inches, 215 pounds of me, weeping openly in the naked light of the morning sun.

I'm not handling this well. Not well at all.

Near my feet on the kitchen floor is a piece of plastic. It is small in size but miles deep with meaning. I've worn this piece of plastic around my wrist for the last seven months. It's my hospital ID bracelet from the night I was admitted to the hospital for the heart attack.

Moments ago the bracelet broke off and fluttered to the floor. The instant it landed, my heart broke open and tears spilled forward.

I bend down and pick up the bracelet and hold it in the palm of my hand like a lost relic. I stand there for a long moment weeping, staring at the tattered and frayed piece of plastic.

I think back to the reasons why I continued to wear my hospital admittance bracelet. I wore it as a way to remember to be grateful for the second chance at life I had gotten, as a reminder to be appreciative for every moment of my life. Each time I'd see it dangling from my wrist, I'd stop, take a breath in and feel the gratitude roll through me.

But I still can't explain the tears.

Why am I weeping? I ask myself.

I wait and listen. A quote floats to the surface of my consciousness.

"The moth broke out of the cocoon before it was ready to fly. He fell to the floor and died."

The quote reminds me of how many times along the journey of the past seven months I had to start before I was ready. I'm still not ready.

I close my eyes and let the moment wash over me. Then it hits me all at once. All the memories of the heart attack, the fragility, dying...rushing in. The falling off was a metaphoric release of the emotions I'd kept buried away since the day I vowed to burn bright.

I understand the lesson in this moment is to *feel.*

Pain knows no time in the heart. Tears come when they come.

No matter how mindful I've been since the heart attack, how honest I've been about honoring my feelings, there is still grief, fear, sadness, and loss that I have not allowed myself to feel.

But men do that. We do everything we can to not feel.

Men think to feel is to be weak. I realize now that to feel is to be alive.

I let the tears flow unchecked down my face and, just as quickly as they came, they stop. I'm left feeling overwhelmed and relieved, along with a sense of calm and peace. I think about how fleeting life is and how grateful I am to be alive.

That night sleep comes down like a curtain.

I dream that I'm a small boy in Japan standing among the cherry blossoms in full bloom. My teacher holds a cherry blossom in his hand. He tells me a cherry blossom has a short life and the fleetingness of its existence is one of the reasons it is so beautiful. He continues, "If we knew the blossom would last forever, it wouldn't have the same exquisiteness."

He tells me life is the same way. We think we will live forever so we are not aware of how fleeting and exquisite life is.

In my dream these words come to me. Words that I want to remember. Words that I need to remember. I tell myself: *do not forget these words.*

The next day I'm sitting in front of a tattoo artist. At 50, this will be my first tattoo. I want the words—the words from my dream—to be etched on my body as a way to remember them.

The tattoo artist starts to dig the needle into my arm. Twenty minutes later I peer down at my forearm and read the words now tattooed across it.

Life isn't lost by dying.

Life is lost minute by minute,

Day by day, by not really living.

I take a deep, long breath and read the words over again and think: *Words to live by. Words to die by.*

We may move forward in life blindly, stupidly, clumsily, but let us not forget the fleetingness and the gift of life. When we respect and honor how fleeting life is, it gives us the courage to really love…to really live.

I stand, thank the tattoo artist and head out the door. A breath of fresh air greets me. I read the inscription on my arm again. I feel a gust of inspiration swell up inside of me. Reading these words reminds me to be brave, to not waste another minute, to follow the dreams in my heart and really live.

As I walk off into the afternoon sun my last thoughts are how we can't always choose the path we walk, but we can choose how to walk it.

I chose to live, love, laugh.

I hope you'll make the same choice, too.

Chapter 6: A Simple Practice That Saved Me

A few weeks after the heart attack I met with the cardiologist in his office. The main thing I wanted to know is what I could do differently in my life to prevent having another heart attack.

The doctor just told me that healthy people like me are really an enigma when it comes to heart attacks. Most people who have heart attacks have an unhealthy lifestyle, so they're given concrete actions to take: quit smoking, start exercising, eat better, lose weight. But with people who are healthy and in shape, it's much more challenging.

I nod okay and ask, "What should I do?"

He responds, "Just keep doing what you're doing."

I stare at him. "Keep doing what I'm doing? Really? That's all you've got?" I frown, take a breath and look back at him. "There has got to be something else. Doing what I did led to a heart attack. I've got to do something differently."

The doctor repeats the bit about healthy people being an enigma. He then adds that I'm taking a statin, which have been shown to be effective in reducing the risk of death for people who have already had a heart attack.

I feel my pulse quicken, my jaw tighten. *Please tell me you've got more for me than this. I don't want to have another heart attack. I want to give myself every chance at surviving.*

"There has got to be something else!" I repeat.

The doctor pauses, adjusts his glasses and looks up at me. "How are your stress levels?"

"Right now, hearing this, not very good."

The doc starts talking about stress being "pandemic" in today's modern world of high-pressure workdays, long commutes in traffic, raising kids, not enough sleep, trying to make ends meet.

He tells me stress raises your cortisol level and leads to chronic inflammation—a hallmark of heart disease. He finishes by saying that doctors used to think stress was a "soft" risk factor, but recent studies show it actually *doubles* the risk of a heart attack.

After hearing his words, I feel a tinge of relief. Reducing stress is something I can work on. It sits with me a lot better than "keep doing what you're doing and swallow these pills."

At home that night, I get on the computer and start to research information about the dangers of stress. I find article after article that chronicles how detrimental stress is for your health. One study from St. Luke's Mid America Heart Institute jumps out at me, as it found that stress is linked with a 42% higher risk of dying two years after being hospitalized from a heart attack.

It's clear to me I need to find peace amid my hurricane of thoughts. This leads me back to a simple practice that I'd forgotten from a few years back, the simple practice of sitting quietly, legs crossed, hands resting in my lap, and breathing.

The simple practice of meditation.

I first started a version of this practice as a lonely, overweight teenager trying to find his place in the world. At 14, I hadn't found anything that I was good at in life. I didn't know what it felt like to be successful.

The first successes I had were ones that I had already seen over and over again in my mind. Using the practice of creative visualization, I went from quitting football my freshman year in high school to being named MVP of the team my sophomore year.

The results were that dramatic. They were life changing.

I saw the success I wanted in my mind, worked hard, and then an unbelievable transformation would occur.

I continued practicing creative visualization from high school football through college football, to the NFL, to standing on the floor of a sold-out Madison Square Garden during the *American Gladiators* tour. Any success I had in life, I had already seen in my mind first.

But somewhere in my mid-20s, at the height of *American Gladiators*, when we were one of the highest-rated shows in America and being aired in 50 countries, I found myself feeling overwhelmed by an emptiness. I felt like a hollowed-out empty shell of a man.

I had assumed that getting to the NFL or being on TV would somehow create impermeable happiness for myself. I believed that since I had achieved these accomplishments, I'd forever be happy. I was shocked when it didn't work out that way.

I had more success than I ever imagined, but sustained happiness eluded me. I was perpetually unfulfilled. I'd often drink, smoke or medicate to relieve my unrest and feelings of emptiness. *It's almost as if the quest of happiness became the root of my unhappiness.*

This is when my creative visualization evolved to meditation. I needed to find a way to ground myself—to steel myself as the world moved rapidly around me. I needed to find a way to be happy and at peace that wasn't reliant on what I accomplished or what I ingested or inhaled.

I realized I had been chasing happiness when the key to happiness was hiding in plain sight. To access it, I simply had to look inward.

I found peace and contentment through meditation—the simple act of sitting, breathing, and emptying my mind.

I was drawn to the simplicity of Zen meditation and the practice of living from moment to moment, in the here and now. I found that whenever I'd sit long enough my anxiety and unhappiness would disappear. I would focus on my breathing and posture, let go of my ego and a sense of peace would come over me.

During meditation there was also a clarity and a connection to all positive qualities of consciousness: love, creativity, intelligence, happiness, energy, power, and peace.

I felt surrounded by love. I felt at home.

Meditation has helped me deal with a lot of my issues. I still felt all the same emotions, but they would pass through me more easily. I wouldn't get stuck on an emotion. I'd feel it, acknowledge it, be with it, then let it go.

When we are worried or anxious, we are too tightly attached to the results we want, rather than doing our best and accepting whatever might happen.

When we are frustrated with someone, it's because we are attached to how we desire him or her to be, rather than accepting that person as the beautiful, flawed human they are.

Dropping attachments is one of the key elements of meditation. It's related to a Buddhist concept called "impermanence". We live in a world that is constantly changing. We suffer because we hold on to things that don't last. When we let go of our attachments and accept things as they are, we let happiness in.

Meditation was the path to finding the light within myself.

But for some reason in the years leading up to the heart attack, I let my practice slip and only meditated occasionally. I'm not sure why, since I found such great comfort and peace in the practice. I guess...sometimes we need to get lost to find our way.

After the heart attack, I returned to meditation. Almost immediately I felt the all positive qualities of consciousness return and grow more and more each day. On the flip side the negativity began to recede. The stress, tension, anxiety, worry, sorrow, anger, and fear all began to lift.

As they lifted, I experienced a great sense of personal freedom, brightness, and peace. I got more happiness out of doing things. I wasn't as attached to results. I had more energy for work and I slept better. I felt healthier and more comfortable in my body and in life. The whole world just looked better.

Each day when I sit in silence and stillness, and breathe and let go of my thoughts, I'm awash in gratitude and appreciation for life. It is here that I believe all things are possible. It is here that I feel a connection to all living things.

It is here that I know love.

It is here that I'm free.

Daily meditation has made a huge difference in my life. There are many things that saved me and helped me be happier and live better. Meditation might be the most important.

If you want to be happier, have less stress, be more at peace, and generally want an overall better quality of life, try meditation.

There are many forms of meditation. Read, research, practice and find one that works for you and do it every day. I've included more information on how to meditate in the appendix.

If you don't do anything else, please try meditation. It will make a difference.

Chapter 7: Lift People Up

It's a brisk March Saturday in Southern California. Sunlight filters in through the window of the cramped gym; barbells and athletes are littered across the floor.

I'm huddled in a corner with Michelle.

I look her squarely in the eyes and say, "You got this. You can do this."

I can see her belief waiver.

I repeat, "You got this. You can do it."

Michelle nods. "Yep...." But I can hear the doubt in her voice. She looks at me one last time and takes a narrow breath as if she's trying to siphon in some of the confidence and belief that I have in her.

A timer counts down. Three...Two...One. Go!

All hell breaks loose as 30 athletes grab their barbells loaded with weights and begin hoisting them over their heads. It's a symphony of grunts and groans mixed with the clanging of iron.

Welcome to the CrossFit Open—a series of gut-busting, stamina-sapping, strength-sucking workouts specifically designed to test your fitness. The best of the best at the CrossFit Open and Regionals will go on to compete in the ultimate test of fitness—the CrossFit Games.

The competitors today at CrossFit Horsepower range in skill from beginners to elite athletes. Each person is competing as an individual, but it feels like everyone is all in it together—like we are all on the same team. The camaraderie and community are amazing. I haven't seen or felt anything like this since back in the days when I played football.

Michelle clangs down her barbell and heads to the pull-up bar. There, she pauses and looks up at the daunting task in front of her.

Michelle will have to do something she has never done before—a muscle up. It's one of the toughest moves in CrossFit, generally reserved for gymnasts, not for regular folks with 9-5 jobs.

A muscle up starts by hanging from a pull-up bar by your hands with your arms fully extended. Then you must swing-propel-launch your body up to the top of the pull-up bar, finishing with your waist above the bar with your arms completely straight in a locked-out position.

For Michelle to do her first muscle up during a competition is like climbing a mountain after running a marathon.

A group of us, her judge and cheering section, huddle around Michelle. The intensity spews from every pore in her body as she jumps up, grabs the pull-up bar and starts to slowly swing her body back and forth—then BAM! She explodes, pulls with everything she's got and vaults her body up onto the pull-up bar and extends her arms.

"Yes! Yes! Yes!" I scream as I thrust my arms up in the air and the gym erupts in pandemonium.

Michelle hops down from the bar beaming as we all rush her and celebrate her victory. I suddenly remember that it's not over; that she is in the middle of a workout. I get her attention, direct her back to the bar and tell her she's got more muscle ups to do.

She jumps up on the bar, and like a champ, bangs out two more muscle ups, vaulting her ahead of thousands of other competitors in the worldwide scoring system. After another ten minutes the workout comes to an end.

Michelle, her friends and I glow in the aftermath of her accomplishment. She didn't win the competition but it was still a huge victory. She did something she'd never done before. It took courage, hard work, and determination.

Driving home after the event, I'm still buzzing from Michelle's triumph. I'm shocked by how much it's affecting me. It feels damn amazing. It feels like I was the one who won something today. In fact, helping her crush it today actually felt better than if I had done it myself.

It dawns on me that since the heart attack there has been this ongoing shift in my life where the achievements of the people I've helped have begun to mean more to me than my own achievements.

It's a stunning reversal from my younger days when I would lap up glory like it was oxygen. I needed it to survive. I mistook applause and adoration for love because, as a young man, I didn't know how to love myself. I was only as worthy and as good as what I accomplished.

Today's experience made me think about something I'd read that the Dalai Lama teaches.

"In every human interaction we have, we can choose to make the person happier or less happy."

When I let these words sink in—I mean really sink in—I realize how much power each of us has to make a positive impact on the world, one human interaction at a time. We hold the power to either lift someone up and make them happier or not to.

When I look at human interaction this way the choice is easy.

I choose to lift people up.

I've since instituted a "lift people up every day" policy that has turned out to be genuinely enjoyable and fulfilling. I make it a conscious, daily priority and it has led to a long string of positive interactions.

When you choose to lift people up, you are choosing joy and you will be a beacon of light, a spark that will burn bright in a world that at times can seem very dark.

Lifting someone up can be something as simple as a smile, a hello, opening the door, putting down the phone and saying hi to the checker at the grocery store, or buying coffee for the next person in line at Starbucks. It can be offering encouraging words, a pat on the back, a compliment, or telling someone you believe in them and you know they've got this.

I believe the small acts of human kindness and making the choice to positively affect every person we come across makes a huge difference collectively in our world. The daily goal of being kind is paid forward over and over again.

It creates a ripple effect of generosity. Single acts of being kind and lifting people up inspire more acts of kindness. If someone is kind to you, you feel good and may be inclined to be kind to someone else. It's a domino effect. The scientific name for this chain of altruism is "upstream reciprocity." It's the idea that acts of kindness grow exponentially.

Kindness has also been linked to the release of oxytocin, a hormone related to feelings of warmth and happiness. In other words, when you are kind or lift another person up your brain's reward center lights up, as if you were the recipient of the gift, rather than the giver. It's a helper's high.

Another thing I've discovered with my "lift people up every day" policy is that those closest to you, your family and friends and even those just outside of your intimate circle, need to be lifted up and encouraged repeatedly.

Lifting people up is a practice like saying, "I love you". People like and need to be told again and again.

Tell them they are great.

Tell them you admire them.

Tell them you believe in them.

Tell them they have greatness inside of them.

Our kids and significant others especially need to hear that we're proud of them.

People need constant encouragement. Tell them repeatedly. Tell them whenever you can. Find a way to lift people up. They need to be reminded they have greatness and beauty inside of them.

If you're reading this, I want you to know that I believe in *you*.

I know there is love and beauty and greatness inside of you.

I know *you've got this*…no matter what your *this* is.

If you're struggling and finding it difficult to hear or believe these words, if no one has told you this before, I can promise you, without a doubt, that there *is* greatness and beauty and love inside of you. It might just be buried beneath the disappointments and unmet expectations, but it is there.

Try reading and repeating the words below over and over again with emotional intensity, until they break through your defenses and you feel them.

There is beauty inside of me.

There is greatness inside of me.

There is love and desire and ambition inside of me.

I got this. I got this. I got this.

By putting these thoughts in a continuous loop, you are creating channels of belief and positivity in your brain. Repeat them again and again with emotional intensity, feeling it over and over again. Make it your truth.

It takes time, but you'll notice the changes. There will be more and more beautiful happenings in your life.

If you want to send me an email and tell me that you believe in me, that you know there is greatness and beauty inside of me, I'll be ecstatic to receive it and I'm sure I'll need to hear it. We all need to hear it.

The bottom line is when you lift people up and are kind, you lift yourself up. When you use the word "amazing" to describe your life, you'll know what I'm talking about.

Last thing. Do me a favor. Start this today. Start with one person. Speak from your heart and let them know that you believe in them. Let them know they are amazing. Let them know they are loved. Motivate them to be who they want to be.

The words can be as simple as:

I love you.

I believe in you.

You got this.

Simple words that change lives.

Chapter 8: Love Yourself First

She stands there quietly, lost in her thoughts. I watch her as she helps people before me in line, not talking as she usually does. Normally, when I shop at Trader Joe's I'll choose her checkout line because I love her upbeat personality. I'd seen her quite a few times over the past few years. But I've never seen her like this. Today she seems sad and distant.

When it comes my turn to check out I greet her with a big grin and say, "Hi."

She smiles faintly and says, "Hello" but offers nothing more.

"How yah doing?" I ask.

"I'm okay..."

I can see she's doing her best to function and do her job but she is not okay. I take a moment and watch her as she scans the items in my grocery cart.

She doesn't want to make eye contact.

She doesn't want to engage.

But I've learned what we want and what we need are sometimes two different things. I think about my "lift people up every day" policy, but at the same time I don't want to be nosy or intrusive.

I have a choice to make in this moment. Pull back, withdraw, take out my phone and disengage or reach out and try and connect with the hurting human being standing in front of me.

I decide to probe gently, "What's going on?"

She shakes her head, nothing.

For some reason I blurt out, "Boy trouble?"

I catch myself and realize that you can't assume anything these days and same-sex relationships are quite common, so I quickly add, "Or uh... girl trouble... or... whoever you're dating... I mean relationship issues."

My fumbling of words gets a slight smile out of her as her eyes meet mine for a brief moment giving me the indication that I'm correct.

Again, I can see she doesn't want to talk about it. This stops me because I realize I don't really know her beyond the casual chit-chat we have while she scans my groceries. The length of time I've been coming to Trader Joe's makes me feel like I know her better than I do, and the last thing I want to be is preachy or to pry into her personal life.

But I also know it's the times when we are broken that connect us to our fellow human beings. We may have different jobs and different upbringings but we all know the pain of being alone, the pain of feeling unloved. It's what joins us as humans.

"Hey..." I say quietly to get her attention.

She looks up at me. I proceed delicately as one does when they are offering advice that wasn't solicited.

"I've found that if you *love yourself first* everything else has a way of taking care of itself."

This hits home. Slowly her demeanor changes. She takes in a deep breath, exhales audibly as tears start to fill her eyes.

I continue, "Too often we look out there for love. For someone to give us love—to love us—so we feel loved. If you can love yourself first with everything you've got, everything else has a way of working out."

I can feel her heart open as I speak. Tears spill down her cheeks. After a long moment her eyes find mine.

"Thank you," she says. "I needed to hear that."

There is more I want to share with her. I want to let her know she's not alone. That we all suffer. That we all experience difficult times.

I open up and share with her how I felt after my heart attack.

"When I was down and out one of the things that saved me was telling myself over and over: *I love myself, I love myself, I love myself.* I put it on an endless loop and repeated it throughout the day over and over again until I felt it and believed it."

She wipes away her tears as I speak. I can see the light within her start to shine.

"You need to talk to yourself in a positive way. Start by repeating to yourself: *I love myself... I love myself...* Tell yourself, *I got this.*"

Suddenly a smile breaks through the gloom.

She reaches out and squeezes my forearm and says, "Thank you."

We stand there for a long moment, two people sharing a moment of human truth connected by what it means to be alive.

This is where *real life* is lived.

It's in the moments we let our guards down and open our hearts and reach out and connect with another human being.

It's in the moments we let our conversation shift from being superficial to being authentic and life-affirming.

It's in the moments we let our light shine so it can brighten the darkness others are feeling.

This is what it means to be alive.

This is what it means to really live.

LOVING YOURSELF FIRST

I know it sounds like a cliché—and it's in every self-help book—but no truer words have ever been spoken. Love yourself first and everything has a way of working out.

What you focus on is what you get.

Focus on loving yourself...and you shall receive love.

Too often we look out "there" for love to make us complete. But the more we seek love, the more it eludes us. When we cease trying to earn love or demand it—and instead focus on loving ourselves—love flows into our lives in beautiful ways we could have never imagined.

Our lives improve. Astounding things start to happen. Opportunities arise, amazing people will come into our lives and situations will naturally resolve themselves.

When we love ourselves we shine, and our light attracts people to us.

As human beings, we crave light.

We gravitate towards it.

When we love ourselves first, our light will shine.

The bottom line is: when we love ourselves, life loves us back.

A simple way to start is to focus on things we appreciate about ourselves. When we focus on things we appreciate, it helps unblock the flow of love.

Some people like to make a list. It may be hard at first, but loving yourself is a habit—like working out or playing the piano. By writing out a list, we are creating the music of our lives.

After my heart attack, I wasn't feeling very lovable. I was in a bad place. I felt broken and down. I was miserable, out of my mind—beyond what I've ever known.

The journey back to life began with me groping for my notebook on my nightstand and forcing myself to write down things I appreciated about myself.

Here is what I wrote:

- I lived

- I'm strong
- I'm a survivor
- I'm a good man
- I'm loyal to my friends
- I'm dependable
- I'm giving
- I'm honest
- I'm kind and have a big heart (even though it's been broken)
- I'm grateful
- I'm brave
- I'm a fighter

Whenever I felt down and started to wallow in self-pity, I focused on this list and I focused on loving myself no matter what. I did exactly what I shared with my friend at Trader Joe's.

I started repeating, "I love myself" over and over again on an endless loop—morning, noon and night—until it broke through and I had no choice but to surrender to it and to love myself.

I believe in positive self talk. I believe loving myself is one of the things that saved me, brought me back to life, and gave me the courage to continue.

I first heard about the concept of repeating "I love myself" over and over again from Kamal Ravikant's book *Love Yourself Like Your Life Depends On it.*

I thank him for opening his heart and sharing this gift with the world.

Chapter 9: I'm Glad I Had a Heart Attack

"If the only prayer you said was thank you, that would be enough."
—Meister Eckhart

After finishing a brutal workout at the gym with my young bud Tyler, I hop into his car to catch a ride home since my car is getting worked on at the shop across the street. It's been about two years since I had the heart attack.

Tyler had just found out about my heart attack. For someone 24 years old, I'm sure it sounded like a death sentence. He looks at me like I'm a *Titanic* survivor. Instantly, I feel every one of my 51 years.

"Dude, that must've really sucked having a heart attack."

"Yah, it did suck."

"That's just crazy man. That's terrible. I'm glad you're doing better."

I nod appreciatively, but my answer doesn't sit well with me. He needs to know this.

"You know… having a heart attack did suck in a big way, but I'm also grateful for it."

He looks at me, stunned.

"What do you mean? No way. How could you possibly be grateful for almost dying and going to the hospital and never really being the same?"

I take a breath and gather my thoughts. Suddenly the moment feels enormous.

"Well… I'm grateful I didn't die. Heart attacks and heart disease kill more people than all cancers combined."

A serious but thoughtful look comes over his face. "I guess you could look at it that way. But I wouldn't want a heart attack no matter what."

I nod my head and smile. I'm sure I would have felt the same way at 24. I clear my voice and continue.

"Look, I didn't want the heart attack, but I'm grateful for who I've become because of it. If that makes sense? I came back different, but I'd say also better."

His brow furrows. I can see he isn't 100% clear.

"The heart attack helped mold me into the man I am today. I've grown in character and compassion. Essentially, through the experience of having a heart attack I've become a better man, and for that I'm grateful."

I pause to let him digest this.

"You see, the moment you learn you are going to die, or believe that you might, a profound shift takes place. In an instant you become aware of what really matters."

"Like what?"

"There are a lot of things that suddenly became more important. My family. My friends. Letting go of grudges. Living life to its fullest. Being braver. Not wasting time. Being more authentic. Being in service. Lifting people up."

He thinks about my responses as we pull into my driveway.

"I think one of the biggest things I've learned that's changed my life the most, is to be grateful. I practice gratitude every day and it's changed my life. If I hadn't had the heart attack, I don't think I would have made these shifts in my perspective. And I'm grateful for seeing things with new eyes."

Tyler chews on this for a moment before a look of complete wonder comes across his face.

"Wow, dude. That's deep. I've never thought about it that way."

With that, I smile at him, we fist bump, and I thank him for the ride home. As I watch him back out of my driveway and pull away, I think about the past two years.

It has been wrenching and difficult—but it's also been some of the most beautiful and profound times of my life. The heart attack *did* mold me into who I am today.

Through the heart attack I've awakened to love and explored new depths of gratitude that I hadn't known before. I wouldn't trade that for anything.

I'm a better man.

I'm a better friend.

I'm a better son.

I'm a better brother.

I'm a better father.

When I was younger I was all about gratification and pleasing the senses. I rushed around chasing all of those wants and desires, but rarely felt grateful. I'd hunt for the next bite before I even tasted the last one, and the more I fed those cravings the hungrier I got. I was perpetually unsatisfied.

I didn't understand the difference between gratification and gratitude.

Gratification is fueled by the desire to please our senses. Things we want to see, hear, taste, touch, smell. The downside is, the more we feed our sensorial wants, the more we crave.

Gratification doesn't make us happy or guarantee happiness in our lives.

Gratitude is the feeling of being thankful, counting your blessings, and being appreciative of all parts of your life, both big and small. Gratitude shifts your focus from what your life lacks to the abundance that is already present.

Through the heart attack, I've learned that gratitude and appreciation are the *gateway to happiness.*

The more grateful I am in my life, the more appreciative, the happier I am.

But here's the catch.

Gratitude is not something you *are* but something you *learn.*

Like happiness, gratitude is something that needs to be cultivated. You have to choose to actively practice it by having an "attitude of gratitude."

You can start by simply choosing to be more grateful and looking around your life for things to feel gratitude for. I've also included more tips on gratitude, and my "Gratitude Practices" in the appendix.

Chapter 10: What Kind of Life do You Want to Live?

I thought more about my conversation with Tyler and practicing gratitude, and realized another predictor of happiness is how we frame events and experiences in our lives.

When we learn to see events in a positive and constructive way, we become architects and creators of happiness in our lives.

When you do this your life changes in incredible ways.

To illustrate the point, I'm going to share with you a day in my life. We'll look at it from two different perspectives—then you can decide what kind of life you want to live.

This past Saturday, it was my brother's 40th birthday. We were having a surprise party for him that night in Orange County, which is roughly 60-70 miles from my home in Los Angeles.

Given that it was a Saturday, I decided to make a day out of it by visiting my mother in the morning, then in the afternoon I'd pop into a coffee shop to get some writing work done before heading to my brother's party later that evening.

I figured since it was a Saturday, traffic wouldn't be too bad. I estimated it'd take me about 45 minutes to an hour to get to my mother's house 40 miles away.

The second I get on the freeway it's gridlocked and I'm stuck in bumper-to-bumper traffic. You just can't win when driving the freeways in Los Angeles. It takes me nearly two and a half hours to drive 40 miles to my mother's house. What a nightmare. I begin to question my sanity for making the trip. There were quite a few times during the drive where I almost turned around and went home.

When I visit with my mother, she is a handful. She hurt her back a while ago and now all she does is complain. I love her, but it's hard to handle all of the negativity.

After spending about an hour with her, I rush off to a local coffee shop to work to meet a deadline. As I'm working I feel my stomach tighten with resentment for having to work on a Saturday.

On top of that, I'm hungry, and I'm very particular about what I put in my body, meaning I've got to go find something healthy to eat, which many times turns out to be awful.

After drudging through my workload and chowing down on a meal, I hop back on the freeway and drive another 25 miles to fulfill my family obligation. It takes me another hour to get to the restaurant for the party. By the time I get there I'm awash in frustration.

At my brother's party, it's hard for me to be present. I can't help but think with dread about the long drive home. To make matters worse, it starts to rain, meaning it could take me even longer to get home because we all know Californians can't drive in the rain.

It takes me another 2 hours to drive home. Once I get there, I collapse on the couch. I've been gone for over 13 hours, six of them stuck in my car, driving from one family obligation to another. I'm beat, frustrated, and still resentful about having to work on a Saturday.

All in all, it was a pretty crappy day that I wouldn't wish on anyone.

Who wants to spend a Saturday cooped up in their car, stuck in traffic driving from one family obligation to next?

It would have been easy to see the day this way.

But let me share with you a different way to look at the same day.

Remember what you look for in life is what you find. When you make gratitude and appreciation your default, you start to see things a different way.

The Same Day Seen in a Different Way

The second I hit the freeway to go to my brother's 40th birthday party, I can see that it's gridlocked. I check Google Maps and it tells me the 40-mile drive is going to take two hours.

Cool.

There is this podcast I've been trying to find time to listen to, and now I've got plenty of time to sit back and enjoy it without being interrupted. I value learning and am grateful for the free time to learn something new.

I arrive at my mother's house. I love her and appreciate her. She's been in a lot of pain lately and wakes up a few times every night crying. Today she tells me she slept through the night for the first time in a while. This is *great* news. I'm happy for her.

After visiting my mother, I pop into a coffee shop to work on a last-minute deadline. I find the perfect, cozy table, tucked in the back of the coffee shop. Score! I feel fortunate the table is available in this busy place.

While working, I realize how lucky I am to be my own boss and to create my own schedule. I'm grateful for the opportunity to be able to write and be in a position to influence and make a difference in people's lives. I'm also proud of myself for having the discipline to do the work on a Saturday and not procrastinate. This is a win.

When I get hungry, I happen to find a lunch spot nearby that has an amazing salad. It was so good that I almost ordered another one in case the food at my brother's birthday party wasn't good. This is *great.*

On the way to my brother's birthday party, my 28-year-old son calls me for no reason at all but to say hello. It doesn't happen often. This is awesome and makes me smile from ear to ear.

When I get to the restaurant for my brother's party, I find a parking space upfront, even though the parking lot is jam-packed. Woohoo! My lucky day.

At the party, my brother announces that he has quit smoking. Today was the first day in 20 years he hasn't had a cigarette. This is amazing in so many different ways!

For my brother's 40th birthday present, I give him our late father's Rolex watch that our dad gave me before he passed away 15 years ago. I knew it meant a lot to my brother, and I felt like now was the right time to pass it on to him. It was a wonderful and great moment where we were connected in a more meaningful way then we had in years.

At the party, I have the good fortune to see all eleven of my nieces and nephews. Nothing fills my heart more than their bright, shining smiles. On top of that, Colton, my two-year-old bruiser of a nephew, crashes into my arms and says my name for the first time. Amazing.

During the course of the party there were other moments when I felt grateful and appreciative, like watching my younger sister Debbie beam with pride as she talked about and showed pictures of the coffee shop she is opening. It was heartwarming. I'm so happy for her.

It's great to see my youngest sister Michelle. I've been fortunate enough to have her work full time for me for the past three years. It's given me a chance to get to know her better than I ever have before. I'm grateful for how close we've gotten.

I look at my other sister Christine. I'm so proud of the strong woman she has become. I'm grateful that she lives close to our mother and is so devoted to taking care of her.

At the end of the night, my siblings and I take our traditional picture and I'm still the tallest. I'm not sure why this still makes me smile, but it does.

Looking at the picture I realize how much I love my brothers and sisters and how blessed I am that we are all healthy and get to spend time together.

Driving home that night I happen to catch Howard Stern's interview with Bill Murray. I've been a fan of his since *Saturday Night Live* and "*Caddyshack.*" It's awesome getting to hear him on Stern. The time flies by and I am home before I know it.

When I walk into my house after being gone for 14 hours I'm greeted by the wagging tails of my two pups. They jump on me and smother me with face licks as I collapse onto the couch.

Sitting there, with these bundles of furry joy, I think about what a wonderfully fulfilling day it was. Throughout the day, I felt a wide range of positive emotions. I felt love and connection. I felt lucky, appreciative, grateful, proud, generous, kind, fulfilled, happy and joyful. I also educated myself with the podcast and felt like I was in service.

All in all, it was an amazing day! And in quite a contrast to the previous example.

What was the difference?

Simple.

I made the choice to see events in a positive and constructive way. I searched for the good moments. I led with an attitude of gratitude. Remember, what we seek is what we find.

When we start with gratitude and appreciation in our hearts, we will find things to be grateful and appreciative of.

I wish I could tell you every day is like this and that I am an unflappable pillar of happiness and calm. I'm not. I'm just like you. I get angry, frustrated and flustered. I act out.

But when I'm living in accordance with who I aspire to be, the good days full of gratitude, happiness and appreciation greatly outnumber the bad days, and my life is good.

It's up to you what kind of life you want to live.

You don't need to be Mother Teresa or the Dalai Lama to start.

You just need to decide.

Chapter 11: Adults Need Recess Too

"The opposite of play is not work—it's depression."
~Anonymous

As my life started to return to normal, the obligations and responsibilities poured back in. I found myself buried between running a company, writing a book, working on speaking engagements and training to qualify for the CrossFit Games.

On top of that I was dutifully working every day to fully live, meditate, and have kindness in my heart. I was practicing gratitude, appreciation, lifting people up and all the things/acts I believe make a life worth living. And even though I was feeling more fulfilled than I had in a long time, sitting at my desk that morning, I still can't help but feel like something was missing.

For lunch I decide to go to the neighborhood park to clear my head. I sit on a bench in the glow of a warmly lit afternoon and do a sort of self-inventory.

I'm grateful for surviving the heart attack, I have love in my life, good friends, satisfying work, peace of mind, kindness in my heart, and the best relationship with my son that I've had in years. All in all, life is good, but I still can't shake this feeling that I am missing something, something that was knocking on the door of my subconscious.

Sitting in the afternoon sun, I take a deep breath in, exhale and listen.

I can hear my heart beating, the wind rustling through the hedges behind me, the sounds of the birds in the trees.

Then I hear:

Laughter. Giggles. Shrieks of joy.

I stand up and move around the giant hedge to find the source of the laughter and walk smack into a five-year-old boy's super hero-themed birthday party in all its glory.

I spot Batman, Superman, Supergirl, Wonder Woman, Harry Potter, Teenage Mutant Ninja Turtles, Star Wars characters and more.

I remark to one of the parents, "Wow. Looks like a party!" She smiles, shrugs her shoulders like she has her hands full. I recognize one of the parents from the neighborhood and we chat for a moment.

I'm just about to leave when Superman tugs on my hand.

"You wanna play?" he asks.

"Oh... no. I can't. I've got to get back to work."

But the little kid is persistent. He keeps tugging on my hand. Soon a Teenage Mutant Ninja Turtle joins him; I know his father from the neighborhood, too.

"Mr. Dan, come and play with us," he pleads.

"You can be the bad guy," says Superman.

"But I don't have a costume," I protest.

Suddenly Harry Potter waves his wand at me. "Abracadabra. You're Lord Voldemort!"

I look down at their hopeful faces. I guess it couldn't hurt to stay for just a few minutes. Suddenly, I feel myself start to transform into the evil Lord Voldemort. I do it in a *Walking Dead* zombie-taking-over-my-body kind of way. I slowly raise my hands out in front of me, pretending my fingers are claws, and let out an unearthly, monstrous roar.

The kids all shriek and run for cover in the safety of the playground's slides, swings and forts. I walk toward them like a zombie thinking this is easy money. I've just scared these kids. My work is done here.

That's when Superman jumps down from the slide and attacks me with a karate chop. I pretend like he momentarily stuns me. Spiderman and the other superheroes spring into action.

All the kids converge on me. I'm like Godzilla walking with one kid attached to my leg, another on my arm, and still another on my back.

I pretend that I'm mortally wounded and fall to the ground, thinking the game will be over and I can get back to work—when Harry Potter suddenly brings me back to life with his sorcerer's wand and the cycle starts again.

It goes on for about 20 minutes—me turning into a monster, the kids shrieking and running, then turning around and attacking me and taking me to the ground.

I have the time of my life.

There is unbridled laughter. There are uninhibited screams of joy.

For a moment, I feel that I've recaptured the lost innocence of childhood and I'm brought back to a simpler time when life was about having fun and enjoying ourselves.

Yes, I think to myself, this is *it*. This is exactly what I was missing.

After the heart attack, I had quickly again fallen into the trap of becoming a human *doing* instead of a human *being*. Everything had gotten so serious with the stress of work deadlines, running a business, paying the bills and the daily demands of a go-go-go life.

I had forgotten to *play.*

When I played with the kids there was a feeling of freedom and fun that had been missing in my life. The experience made me realize how important play is in our lives—not only as kids but also as adults.

I believe in hard work, dedication, and discipline, but I also think somewhere along the line we have lost our way. We pride ourselves on how long and hard we can work. We skip vacations, we work morning, noon and night, at home, on the road, and when we are having family time with our kids.

We've gotten it terribly wrong.

Instead of *working to live…we live to work.*

This isn't healthy.

Play matters.

As grown-ups, we need recess too. It's a critical component to living a happy and fulfilled life. According to Dr. Stewart Brown, author and director of the National Play Institute, "Nothing lights up the brain like play." Brown has spent decades studying the importance of play. His research shows that play relieves stress, releases endorphins, improves brain function, stimulates the mind and boosts creativity, improves relationships and connections to others.

In his book *Play*, Dr. Brown calls play a catalyst: "A little bit of play can go a long way toward boosting our productivity and happiness."

But how do we add more play to our lives?

First, we need to define "play." The general definition is something that is done for its own sake. It's voluntary, it's pleasurable, it offers a sense of engagement, and it takes you out of time. And the act itself is more important than the outcome.

In simpler terms, it's letting loose and having fun. It's not taking yourself so seriously. It's connecting with the childlike part of yourself where you are completely detached from your surroundings.

What constitutes play and having fun are different for everyone.

For me it involves a lot of sports or outdoor activities: tennis, basketball, softball, ping pong, golf, tossing the football, paddle boarding, kayaking, biking, and hiking.

It can be playing foosball, going to an arcade, miniature golf, batting cages, checkers, chess, board games, kickball, dodge ball or darts.

Playing with little ones is a huge source of fun for me. It helps me experience the magic of play through their experience. I've had dogs for most of my life, from purebreds to mutts. I've loved them all. They are another huge source of play and fun in my life.

As I reviewed my list of activities that were fun and thought of as play, I wondered if I could add CrossFit to the list. It's something I do every day that I look forward to, it is voluntary and offers a sense of engagement.

But the act of pushing my body to the limit until I'm huddled in the fetal position on the ground in a puddle of sweat certainly isn't fun. It is gut-wrenchingly hard work, and perhaps testing fate with my heart history.

But CrossFit also provides novelty by forcing you to learn new skills such as gymnastics; in addition, there is a new workout every day and it takes strategizing to figure out how to best complete it.

But viewing the excruciating workouts of CrossFit as play?

Oh, no, no, no, they are not fun.

Many times in the middle of a grueling workout I want to quit and ask myself: Why the hell am I doing this? But each time when I finish and come out on the other side, I feel cleansed and baptized by the fire and adrenaline that only a hard workout can bring.

But fun? Play? Not a chance.

Then it struck me—what is fun about CrossFit isn't the workouts but the camaraderie. It is the time before, after, and in between, when I am laughing, joking and goofing around with like-minded people who quickly became friends.

In a bigger sense, CrossFit fulfills more than just having fun—it fills the needs of human connection, belonging and community.

It's the same reason I loved playing sports.

Sports taught me about life.

Almost dying taught me how to live.

Part of really living is to play more and have fun. The number one regret of dying people is that they wish they hadn't worked so much.

Don't make this mistake.

Ask yourself this question. If I was given one more day to live, what fun thing would I make sure to do?

Whatever you come up with, go and do it now.

Find your fun.

Live fully and play more.

Time isn't guaranteed.

Chapter 12: Spandex Rules

It hadn't seen the light of day in 20 years.

I'm not sure how I ended up in possession of it, nor am I sure why I even kept this little red, white and blue keepsake, bedazzled in sequins.

It's made out of spandex.

The word "Nitro" is written down the right leg.

It's my uniform from the TV show the *American Gladiators.*

Being an American Gladiator is a part of who I am and I've got a lot of great memories—but the ridiculous outfit was something I was embarrassed of and didn't like wearing.

When the American Gladiators did a special episode on the TV show *Family Feud*, I had a prominent scowl on my face because we had to wear the uniforms. During the introductions, the host at that time, Richard Dawson came over to me and asked me if I was mad.

I glared at him and said, "Let me ask you a question. If you were a grown man and had to wear spandex on TV, wouldn't you be mad?"

The audience cracked up. Even Richard laughed and said, "Yes. Yes, I would."

The bottom line was that I had always felt I was more than my spandex—and wanted to be seen as a person, actor, writer, etc. I was young and very serious in those days.

When the show ended, I vowed never to wear spandex again.

This was back then—back before I knew spandex was a privilege not a right.

All joking aside, after I made a commitment to play more and have fun and to not take myself so seriously, I thought perhaps unearthing the spandex would be a good way to cement and celebrate my vow—a coming out party of sorts.

I decided to wear my spandex to the gym for a workout.

Yep, that's right.

I was going to wear my sequined spandex on a regular day at the gym for no reason at all.

That afternoon, I dug deep into the bowels of my garage and excavated my old uniform from a dust-filled box. I wiped back the cobwebs and held the tattered and frayed relic up in the light. Looking at its dilapidated condition, my biggest fear was that the singlet would fall to pieces in the middle of the workout, giving people a view of far more than they wanted to see.

If I'm being honest, that wasn't my biggest fear.

What scared me most was a little voice that whispered to me: *What are you doing? You're going to look like an idiot! Don't do it.*

This voice almost stopped me in my tracks.

It's the day of the workout and I'm sitting in my car in the gym's parking lot for several minutes before going in—and I'm not even wearing my uniform yet.

When I finally go into the gym, I slide into the bathroom and squeeze into the ancient red, white and blue spandex. I stand there looking at my reflection in the mirror. I'm sweating and my heart is banging in my chest.

The little voice keeps whispering, *You look stupid! Nobody cares. They are going to make fun of you. Look at him holding onto the past. Loser. Get a life!*

It's hard to believe that I'm 50 years old. It feels like I am five.

At this point I have two choices. Take the spandex off and go out there in my regular gear and forget my commitment to having more fun and playing. Or walk out there in all my spandexian glory.

I ask myself the simple question: Will it be fun?

I thought that it would.

So I ignore the negative voice, walk out of the bathroom and onto the workout floor. My spandex, after 20 years of hibernation, is on view for all to see.

There are laughs. There are hoots and hollers. There is cheering and jeering.

It is glorious. It is fun.

It feels good to have the spandex on again. *Too good.*

Better than it should feel or than I thought it would.

The experience left me with one thought: *Why in the hell did I wait so long to put the spandex back on?*

As kids we all felt like superheroes at one time and never questioned putting the costume on. We never questioned the world of make believe. We played and had fun and lived in a world where we believed *anything* was possible.

It's time to put the cape back on, look up at the horizon and dare to fly.

Oh, and by the way, my spandex and I are now available for birthday parties and Bar Mitzvahs!

Chapter 13: Use Me, God

I became who I am today in a shower of sparks. I remember the exact moment.

I am 10 years old. My brother Randy is 12.

He is lying in my arms, burnt, bleeding, dying...after being electrocuted. White smoke fills the air with the stench of burnt skin. I'm crying and sobbing. Begging him not to die.

I notice his fingers. They have been burnt to stubs. Fragments of white bone are visible through the charcoal-black flesh that extends all the way up to his wrists.

We are alone.

I'm scared...I do not know what to do. I'm holding him...hugging him...loving him... needing him...not wanting to let go of him.

Yet, I know I need to leave him to try and save him.

I rush out of the house to the street to find help, leaving my dying brother alone. I spot two city workers on the street and beg them for help.

We charge into the house. They pull my brother away from the electrical wires and lay his rigid body on the floor. My eyes flick across the workers as they check his vitals. I'll never forget the sickening hum of electricity coursing through my brother's body. It sounded like a swarm of a thousand bees.

I keep asking them if he's alive.

The men don't respond and continue frantically to check my brother's body.

Suddenly one of the men says, "We need to take him to the hospital." My heart jumps. Even at 10 years old I know that means he is still alive and there is something worth saving.

I rise and stand over my brother, looking down at him. His face is undamaged and still beautiful, but his charred body is rigid. I know there is a word for this... rigor... rigor... something... but isn't that only after someone has been dead for a while?

With the men's help we get my brother to the hospital.

At the hospital, while the doctors work on my brother, I pummel my fists into a wall in a blind rage, pleading with God, don't let my brother die. I pray to God to take me instead of him. I feel my brother Randy is the one who deserves to live, not me.

He is stronger, smarter... better than me.

I weep and beg God.

"Please God take me. Take me instead of my brother."

I bang my fist into the wall over and over again asking God repeatedly.

> *"Please God take me. Take me instead of my brother. Please take me."*

I need my brother.

I can't go on without him.

I won't make it.

Regardless of my prayers, my brother dies a few hours later.

That would be the last time I prayed.

At 10 years old, I lost my faith in God. I lost faith in the idea that there was a benevolent force that watched over us and listened to us and helped us. I believed if there were a God, he wouldn't have let my brother die.

My brother was my rock. My hero. My idol. I was comfortable in his shadow.

Losing him *devastated* me.

I felt alone in the world.

Abandoned.

Through our parents' divorce, moving from family to family, school to school, home to home, state to state, country to country, my brother was the one constant. He was with me every step of the way.

I miss him to this very day.

Forty years later and after my heart attack, I start to pray again.

Being in touch with my mortality connected me to a higher source.

Back when I had the heart attack, I remember being wheeled into the hospital by the paramedics and floating above my body. I was in a great, golden light and experienced myself as a transparent, radiant energy.

I looked down at the people below me and saw that each person had the same light and brilliance emanating from them. They were like stars shining bright, connected by one thing.

LOVE.

All races.

All religions.

All classes.

All sexualities.

CONNECTED BY LOVE.

In that moment, I knew and felt God in the most intimate sense.

God is love.

Love is what connects us all.

That was a cathartic revelation. Bathed in the bright light of acute clarity, I saw clearly. I realized without God there can't be love, beauty, honor, virtue, hope, redemption or grace. Science has no explanation for them. There has always been a gap in scientific theory when it comes to explaining the core fundamentals of the human experience.

My concept of God changed. It's not an antiquated view where a bearded man in robes sits on a throne looking down and watching over us. It's not confined to religious concepts or based on exclusion of those who have different beliefs.

It is simple.

God is love.

Love is God.

I feel God every day in my life when I feel love, beauty, grace, and kindness.

There is comfort here. There is peace.

I know when people face death they often pray and turn to God out of fear and for salvation. When I pray now, I don't pray for God to watch over my soul in case it is the only way into heaven. I don't pray to God to save my life or help me survive. I don't pray for material things or for a better life.

Each time I pray, I say the same prayer.

I say this prayer toward the end of my meditation when I've quieted the voices in my head, cleared my mind, and I feel a deep connection to God.

I pray the same prayer that Martin Luther King Jr. prayed.

Use me, God.

Show me how to take who I am...

Who I want to be...

What I can do...

And use it for a purpose greater than myself.

When I was dying I felt a divine bliss inside of me—a deep connection to every person and living being on the planet. In this connection there was love and abundance and humanity.

The connection was so strong that I was left with the deep desire to be in service.

I believe when we give to others, we give to ourselves. When we share our unique gifts, however large or small, when we burn bright, we generate significance and create the circle of our destiny.

This prayer brings me back to center. It gives me a place to start. It opens up my heart to all the possibilities of goodness and being in service.

Being in service is something I vow to do every day.

It's often in random acts of kindness. Opening the door for a stranger, letting someone who is in a hurry go in front of you in line, grabbing something off the shelf for a person who can't reach, helping a fellow passenger get their luggage down from the overhead bin on a plane.

You don't have to pray to be in service.

You just need to have kindness in your heart.

I can tell you this. I've never regretted an act of kindness.

I've never regretted praying or meditating.

I believe everyone should follow their own faith and practices. However, if this prayer—these word—resonates with you, try it on for size and see how it shifts your perspective. When you open your heart to being in service, your life changes.

Chapter 14: Play that Funky Music

Work like you don't need the money. Love like you've never been hurt.

Dance like nobody's watching.

~ Satchel Paige

I'm a bit scared to share this one. You are going to think I've lost it, but one of my favorite happiness hacks is to bring in the funk and move my junk.

Anytime.

Any place.

Anywhere.

That's right. I'm talking about taking dance breaks.

Before my heart attack, dancing was something I reluctantly did at weddings, and only after having the magical elixir booze. When I went out on the floor, I'd always feel a bit self-conscious. I'd worry if I was on beat or if I looked like I was having a seizure or if I was a weird guy who thinks he can really dance, but can't.

We all know that guy—he's at every wedding. Right?

Well, guess what? Part of cultivating happiness is throwing caution to the wind and letting loose and being *that* guy or girl.

There is something about moving your body to the rhythm of the boogie of the beat that can't help but make you feel invigorated and alive.

It doesn't matter if it's the Electric slide, Macarena, Moonwalk, Two-step, *Footloose*, *Flashdance,* or your own crazy moves. Who hasn't thrown caution to the wind and gotten lost in the rhythm of the boogie of the beat?

Whenever I've been sitting at my desk for too long, when I'm feeling down, when I need a lift and all the caffeine in the world won't perk me up, I turn on my stereo and put on a favorite song and start to bust a move.

Now, I'm not a good dancer. I don't have any moves and I certainly can't twerk.

But that's not the point.

The point is to start moving your body and do the funky-funk.

My favorite old school jam is "Play that Funky Music" by Wild Cherry.

From the time the first beats roll in, I'm already feeling the groove overtake my body. I can't help but give over to the beat. To the funk.

My head starts to bop. My shoulders groove back and forth. Then it goes to my hips. They move and grind in ways that would make many moms scream, cover their kids' eyes and leave the room.

But I don't care, because I can feel the funk take over my body. I let it go. I'm not concerned about what anyone thinks. I sing every word on the track like I'm up on stage on Soul Train. My mouth forms a circle shape and out comes a guttural, "Owwwww..."

Here comes the guitar solo. I break out the air guitar amidst the funk. As the song goes on, out come the jazz hands.

What? Wait-wait-wait! Jazz hands???

I've completely lost my mind now. The hands go up over my head and my whole body sways to the music. This is the power of the funk. I dare you to play this song and not feel the funk come grooving in.

As soon as the first notes hit the airwaves, I start to get funky.

The good kind. The groovy kind. The kind where my head starts to bob and my shoulders start to move on their own. Then it's the hips. I'm funking out in an evil way.

I keep the gesticulating genius going until the song ends. Each time I finish, I feel invigorated, alive and free. Sometimes, I'll put the song on loop and let it play over and over again. Whatever it takes to shake the blues and put myself in a happy, positive uplifted state.

Yes, it can be tiring. And yep, you might pull a muscle.

But you can't put a price on happiness and feeling good.

And it's not just me saying that doing the funky-funk will help you cultivate happiness.

Dancing is a form of exercise that is known to release endorphins. It also causes our brains to secrete the "bonding" hormone oxytocin, known as the "happy" or "love" hormone.

Dancing also brings us back to a more primitive and liberated state of mind. It causes thoughts to simplify, to focus on our bodies and movements instead of the complicated stressors in our lives.

The key is to really let loose during your dance break. You don't need to be a good dancer—I'm certainly not—you only need to give over to the funk and beat and let yourself go.

Forget what you look like. Don't compare yourself to others. Having fun and busting a move should be your top priority.

Make your mantra self-expression, not comparison.

If you don't have a favorite song to jam to, try "Play That Funky Music." It'll get you out of your chair and grooving and getting down to the rhythm of the boogie of the beat. Owwwww!

Take that dance break. You'll thank me after.

WARNING: May be habit forming and even contagious!

Chapter 15: Your Secret Weapon

What if I told you that you have a secret weapon, one that can make tremendous change in your life, one that you are not using nearly enough?

You were born with it.

It doesn't cost anything to use.

You don't have to learn anything to use it.

It can only be used to do good.

And it's been scientifically proven to make you happier.

Would this be something you'd be interested in?

Research confirms that when you use this secret weapon, it sends a message to your brain that lights up your reward center in a way that even chocolate, a well-regarded pleasure inducer, cannot match.

Two scientists did a 30-year study at UC Berkeley in California showing that people who used their weapon the most in their college yearbook pictures had better marriages, fewer setbacks and were generally happier in the following 30 years.

In another study published in the journal *Psychological Science,* researchers at Wayne University found that baseball players who used their secret weapon more intensely lived seven years longer than those who did not.

Researchers also found using your secret weapon reduces anxiety as well as lowers your blood pressure and heart rate.

The odd thing is that, as we get older, we stop using this secret weapon. Children use it up to 400 times a day while the average adult only uses it 20 times a day.

What is this "secret weapon"?

Your smile.

If there was ever a magic pill for happiness, this might be it.

With this simple tool we can alter our brain's emotional pathway to feeling happier.

When you smile you contract the main two smiling muscles: the zygomatic major (raising the corners of the mouth) and the orbicularis oculi (raising the cheeks). When these muscles contract they fire a signal to your brain that stimulates your reward center by creating endorphins.

When our brain feels happy and endorphins are produced, it signals back to your facial muscles to smile. The smile, in return, once again creates endorphins.

In short, when our brain feels happy, we smile. And when we smile, our brain feels happy. It creates an endless loop of positive feelings.

You feel happy. You smile.

You smile. You feel happy.

Be mindful. Only a genuine smile creates happiness. The fake smile, or what scientists call the "social smile," occurs when we only smile with our mouth corners and fail to contract the orbicularis which raises the cheeks and causes eye crinkling.

Another thing about your smile is that when you unleash it on a person they have no choice but to smile back! When you smile at them it triggers mirror neurons in their brain that automatically causes them to return the smile.

Smiling is contagious. Try it.

If there's someone next to you right now, smile at them and see if they smile back. If you're alone, try smiling and see if it triggers feelings of happiness.

Make sure it's a genuine smile. Remember only a genuine smile triggers happiness.

Did it work?

I was curious as well, so I decided to do an experiment to test the theory of the power of the smile and its effect on our happiness.

It also got me wondering how many times a day I smiled and if the frequency made a difference in my level of happiness. Was I like the average adult who only smiled 20-25 times a day? Or more like a kid who smiled on average 400 times a day?

On the test day I decided to count the number of times I smiled by carrying a little clicker in my pocket. For the day, I also instituted a "smile at everyone I encounter" policy.

Walking around Los Angeles smiling at everyone I came across had interesting results. In L.A., people are generally warmer than people in Manhattan to a degree, but there isn't that hometown feel of the South or Midwest where people you don't know actually stop and talk to you and listen to what you have to say.

Having a smile plastered to my face generally resulted in people smiling back at me.

I'd say I had about a 75 percent success rate.

The interesting thing was when someone smiled back at me, there was this innate urge to smile back again, creating an endless loop of smiles that can either be endearing and get you date propositions...or put you on people's "creepy dude" alert.

This result is backed up by a study at Uppsala University in Sweden that found when we see people smile, it stimulates mirror neurons and triggers a smile from us in return.

One of the best things that happened on my “smile at everyone I encountered day” was that I felt happier. There was a general overall improved sense of wellbeing. I had quite a few of my acquaintances say things like:

“Seems like someone is in a good mood today.”

“You seem happier than usual.”

I noticed that when I was happier, it lifted people up and made them a little happier too.

I also discovered this gladiator smiles a heck of a lot.

I counted 232 times that day.

The results might be skewed because every time I thought about counting my smiles it made me smile, and then when I clicked the clicker in my pocket it made me smile again.

It was an unexpected benefit.

A smile has power. It knows no language barrier, no demarcations of race, gender or class. It's the one thing that is truly universal among humans.

Mother Teresa said:

> *"We shall never know all the good that a simple smile can do."*

A lot of people think one person can't make a difference in the world. I believe our impact is far greater than we know and that one person can absolutely make a huge difference.

You can be an agent of change in the world by doing many of the things in this book including smiling more. When measured against the vastness of the world it may seem insignificant, but to the people you lift up, the significance can be profound.

When you make the choice to genuinely smile more, it makes you happier.

When someone sees your smile it makes them happier.

It creates a ripple effect of happiness.

So, pull out that smile, be an agent of change for those around you, and promote happiness and positivity in a world starved for it.

Start now. Smile more.

Chapter 16: What You Do Is Not Who You Are

I knew this guy in high school who scoffed at taking a typing class because he was sure he would have a secretary taking dictation for him. He was a guy who went to college to play football and meet girls.

This guy had probably read only a handful of books in his life by the time he finished college. Truth be told, he didn't finish college after all that talk...he left when his football scholarship ran out.

The most he'd written in his life was a term paper. He wasn't well-read and he certainly wasn't a storyteller.

So why am I telling you about him? Something happened to this guy in his early 20s.

He suddenly felt he had stories inside of him that he wanted to tell. Thoughts and ideas spilled forward that he had to get out. He didn't know how to type, so for eight weeks, every morning, he practiced on the computer until he could type 50 words a minute.

Now he could type, but he still didn't have any idea how to write. So this guy went out and bought and studied every book he could find on writing—and he began to write every day.

He also became a voracious reader—reading 40-50 books a year.

He felt screenplays were the best medium for him because there were more ways to hide his inability in writing in the screenplay format. There isn't a lot of description, just short tags to show the setting. Plus, he could fill pages easier due to the formatting of screenplays, in which the dialogue takes up large chunks.

He wrote every day for seven years before he finally had success and sold a script.

He eventually sold a few more...and two of his scripts were actually made into movies.

This guy kept writing screenplays every day for years. He never dreamed of writing a book because that was reserved for the "smart" people. Not him.

But 17 years after he first taught himself to write, he somehow had his memoir published by one of the largest publishers in the world, Simon and Schuster.

He'd finally become a published author.

His editor at Simon and Schuster told him his book was "Triumphant."

The book also got great reviews by some of the most revered writers of our times who said amazing things about his work.

He also had people who bought the book tell him how his words changed their lives—how it was one of the best books they'd read—and thanked him for being brave enough to write it.

But less than a year after his book was published, he QUIT writing.

Why?

Because his book didn't sell as many copies as he thought it would.

He was embarrassed.

Ashamed.

Disheartened.

He threw away 17 years of work because he didn't get the results he wanted. (Btw – his book did actually sell well. It sold more copies than 97% of non-fiction books. But that didn't feel like a success.)

He felt he didn't have the strength to go through the process again. He thought, *why give your all toward something, why work your ass off, if there isn't a pot of gold at the end of the rainbow?*

Well, guess what...

This guy is Me.

When I didn't get the response I wanted, I assumed it was because I wasn't a good writer and chalked it up to the notion that nobody cared.

I put all my value and self-worth on the number of copies I sold.

How could I not?

The book was my memoir. It was about *me*. If people didn't buy my book, it meant they didn't like me. If people didn't buy my book, it meant I must be a bad writer.

So, when the book didn't sell well, according to my definition of success, after 17 years of writing every day, I gave up.

I quit.

I didn't write another word for six years.

Then, after the heart attack, something changed.

I started to feel a stirring in my gut that I still had stories to tell. I felt the need to share what it means to be alive. I wanted to illuminate the human condition.

I wanted to live a life full of purpose, service and gratitude.

I realized I didn't start writing because I wanted to; I started writing because I had to. But somewhere along the way I got lost.

It all became about the results.

I didn't lose my passion. Fear shattered my passion.

Placing all my value on the results shattered my passion.

I didn't see that it was about the effort. I didn't see that it is about happily achieving instead of achieving to be happy.

What I put forth is what I do, but not what I am.

When we base our self-worth on the outcome and how our work is received, we end up buying into a system that is reliant on other people's opinions. When we do that, we've taken our power and given it to others.

I've learned to value being daring, taking a risk and creating. For putting my work out there and letting it live.

I put value in seeing what I can be and do...not on the results.

I realized I wrote because I had to and because I love it. It's my passion and my life's work. My happiness isn't measured by how the work is received. My happiness comes from creating and putting my work out in the world with the hopes that it will inspire and change lives.

Don't get me wrong, I still want people to love, respect and possibly admire what I've created, but my self-worth is not based upon what people think of my work.

Yes, it's disappointing when we don't reach our desired goals. It's hard when our achievements aren't met with the excitement we had hoped. But I've learned that I am not who I am based on the sales of a book or how much weight I can lift.

Regardless of how many books I sell, speeches I give or likes I get on social media posts, I know that I am a good man. I have a big heart. I do good things. I'm a father. I'm a brother, uncle, son, partner, and a good and trusted friend.

This is who I am.

It took me a long time to realize this. I still struggle with it.

But take it from me: you are more than what you do. What you do is what you do, not who you are. Have boldness in your heart. Find your place in the world. Don't let anyone's opinion keep you from being you—or keep you from shining.

You are the best and only you on the planet.

Chapter 17: Do What Scares You

The view couldn't be better.

The white-sand Hulopoe Bay beach stretches on for an eternity. Gentle waves lap against shoreline. The island of Lanai is only nine miles from Maui yet a world away.

It is the perfect off-the-beaten-path getaway I was looking for.

The hotel is located on a picturesque bluff above Hulopoe Bay. It's early. I'm in the hotel gym, running on the treadmill as a way to shake off the jet lag and start my day off right. The beach below me is still empty as I watch the sun start to rise, spraying light on the tropical paradise below.

My eyes are drawn to movement in the water 50 yards from the shore.

I hop off the treadmill and rush over to the gym attendant, Russell.

“Hey Russell, is that a fin in the water?”

The bear of a man glances out at the water. “Yep,” he says casually with a thick Hawaiian accent.

“Is it a shark? I’m terrified of sharks. The movie *Jaws* did me in years ago.”

He chuckles. “No brah. Spinner dolphins. We have the largest population of spinner dolphins in the world.”

I look back out at the water. It’s far enough below that I can’t see it 100% clearly. “Are you sure? I’m frickin’ terrified of sharks.”

He points to the ocean. “Look. You can see other fins out there too. It’s definitely a school of dolphins.”

I study the water closely and see he is correct. There are roughly fifteen fins breaking the surface.

“Cool! I love dolphins. I’ve always wanted to swim with them.”

“You should go down there and do it then.”

“Really?”

He nods his head, yep. “They don’t come here often. It’s a sign from the gods.”

That would be amazing. I love dolphins and to be able to swim with them in the open water would be incredible. But, on the other hand, I’m terrified of sharks. What if there was a shark out there among them, pretending to be a dolphin, until I hopped in the water—then it’s goodbye Gladiator.

I seriously contemplate doing it. I weigh out the risk versus the reward in my mind. Risk: I get eaten by a shark and die. Reward: I get a once in a lifetime experience.

But is this experience worth possibly dying for?

Wait, wait, wait, I tell myself. They are dolphins down there in the bay, not sharks. Sharks are what I pictured in my mind. But dolphins are what all evidence is pointing to. This is what fear is. It’s imagining the worst.

Finally, I decide, *I’m going to do it. I’m going to swim with the dolphins.*

I'm filled with a rush of excitement, but before I run down to the beach and jump in the ocean, I want to make sure that Russell had done it. It would give me that last little bit of extra confidence I needed to overcome my terror of sharks.

"Hey Russell, have you ever swam with the dolphins?"

He looks at me sheepishly. "Nope."

"Why not?"

"Cause I'm afraid," he says as his shoulders slump and he suddenly seems like he's twelve years old.

Unbelievable! This guy was telling me to go out and swim with the dolphins, when he's lived here all of his life, and he's never done it? There is no way I am going out there. If it was safe, he would have done it. There have to be sharks out there.

I jump back on the treadmill and start to run. Light shines across the bay and the empty beach. I can still see the fins in the water, 50 yards from the shore, circling around the surface.

I begin to feel something tightening inside of me.

It is an uneasiness, the feeling that I'm not living my life fully.

If there was anything the heart attack taught me, it was to be a collector of moments, not things. Swimming with the dolphins is one of these moments. Doing it here on the island of Lanai, in the open water of Hulopoe Bay, would be a once-in-a-lifetime experience that I'm not willing to pass up because of fear.

I look at Russell and announce, "I'm going out there, man. I'm going to swim with the dolphins." Russell nods and gives me a thumbs up.

I exit the gym and strut down the concrete path, past the pools, toward the beach. It is still empty except for a lone hotel employee, a rail-thin Hawaiian woman in her 60s, who pokes trash with a wooden pole with a spear on the end of it.

I hit the sand and look out at the vastness of the ocean in front of me. It is suddenly dark and foreboding. I boldly declare to the Hawaiian woman, "I'm going out to swim with the dolphins."

"Good. You should!" she says with an emphatic just-do-it burst of energy. "The dolphins don't come here very often. It's a sign from the gods."

I see the excitement dancing in her soulful eyes. I'm pumped. I have faith. I am completely ready for whatever might come.

Emboldened, I ask her. "Have you ever done it?"

After a long pause she says, "Nope, I'm afraid."

The enthusiasm drains from my body. I feel the doubt creeping back in as I walk to the water's edge. It's eerily calm. Not a wave in sight, just the gentle lapping of the water against the shore. I look out and can still see the fins circling in the water, but now that I'm closer, I realize they are not 50 yards away from the shore. They are over 100 yards away.

I stand there for a long moment waiting for some kind of sign, like one of the dolphins bursting through the surface and leaping into the air like they do at Sea World, so I'd know they are indeed dolphins, not sharks.

I go over my rules for swimming in the ocean because of my fear of sharks. First, I don't go out very far. 100 plus yards is certainly further than I ever go. Second, I don't swim in the early morning or late evening because that's when sharks are known to feed. Third, I don't ever go into the water alone.

If I go out there now, I'll be breaking all my rules about going into the ocean, rules that I've had since I was a teenager and saw the movie *Jaws.*

I stand there frozen on the shore. A thought floats to the surface.

> *If you want to live a life you've never lived, you'll have to do things you've never done.*

I repeat that mantra over and over in my head as I push back my fears, step into the water and start to swim towards the circling fins. The panic sets in when my feet can no longer touch the ocean floor. I'm bobbing up and down in the ocean feeling like a shark shish kabob.

It suddenly occurs to me that I have bright colored shorts on. Another no-no if you don't want to attract a shark's attention. I take in a deep breath, still myself and keep swimming further out. With every stroke the ocean shifts. I am only 60 yards out but the shore seems miles away.

I get the distinct feeling that I do not belong here.

The further I swim out, the further away the circling fins seem to be. I'm not a strong swimmer, and I begin to doubt myself. I think: *I should probably turn around. This is a stupid idea. I'm an idiot for being out here by myself in the water.* Every part of me is telling me, *this is a bad idea and can lead to no good.*

But there is a pulling deep inside of me that is stronger than the fear. Somehow I know I have to keep going. I start to swim again, 10 yards, 20 yards, 30 yards, 40 yards. I am now 150 yards from the shore.

I stop and tread water. I feel like I had reached the place I last saw the fins circling. I scan the surface but don't see anything. It's too quiet. The sky had darkened even more. My eyes shoot to the shore. No one is there. Not even the lady with the soulful eyes.

Great. There is no one to hear my scream.

I start to really panic when something flashes underneath me, followed by a warm rush of water. I feel the presence of something large near me. My eyes dart everywhere trying to assess the situation.

I just *know* it's a shark.

He's scared the dolphins away and now he is going to attack me. I'm going to die out here in the ocean.

My mind races wildly going over my options. I can swim as fast as I can to shore and hope the shark isn't hungry and won't attack me. I can stay where I am and do nothing—and be as scared as hell and probably drown. A part of me thinks that isn't such a bad idea. Sometimes doing nothing is easier than facing your fears.

My last option is to investigate further, so I can make an educated decision. If it *is* a shark, at least I'd know it and can think of a game plan.

I take a deep breath and force myself to go underwater to investigate.

What I see takes my breath away.

It's a fantastic world like no other—awe-inspiring, infinite.

A pod of 20-25 dolphins swims in a circle around me. I am at the very epicenter of the circle; they are 15 feet away as they encircle and surround me. There is a feeling of an unbroken calm in the swarm of movement, speckled by fragments of light from above.

I can see beauty, kindness, and intelligence in their gentle eyes. My fear evaporates. My sense of ego, of separation, melts away and I have a feeling of total connection to what is happening around me.

Suddenly, one of the dolphins breaks from the circle and darts past me, almost as if he is inviting me to reach out and touch him. He rejoins the circle when another dolphin breaks towards me and shoots right past me.

I can't believe it! They're playing a game with me.

The dolphins continue to take turns darting right past, always making sure to stay just out of my reach. I keep coming up for air and going back underneath the surface of the water to see the beautiful creatures.

I know I'm in the presence of something magical—something that few people ever get to experience.

I don't want to leave. I know it's something I'll probably never get to see again, but after 15 minutes there I know it's time for me to go. I still have a long swim to get back to shore. With that thought, I submerge one last time.

A sudden wave of bliss bathes my soul in grace and gratitude. There is a feeling of unity, transcendence, completeness and oneness with all creation. I stay underwater for as long as I can, taking in the beautiful happening around me.

When I can't hold my breath anymore, I come up and start to swim back. When I reach the shore, I turn back and take another look at the ocean.

I want to commit it to memory.

I want to be able to come here in my dreams.

Chapter 18: The Time to be Brave is Now

Sometimes summoning a little more courage is the difference between the life you are living now and the life you want to live. For me, it was the difference between standing on the shore on Hulopoe Bay looking at a life I wanted to live versus living that life.

I pushed past my fears. I pushed past what other people were willing to do in order to experience something breathtaking and exquisite.

Did I go much farther than Russell who worked at the gym or the woman on the beach?

Absolutely not.

It was only 100 to 150 yards.

But in life, going that little bit of extra distance can make all the difference in the quality of your life.

It's easy to stand on the shore and play it safe.

Safe from ridicule. Safe from humiliation. Safe from failure.

But by playing it safe you're missing out on the beauty of life, the richness, the person you were meant to be.

Often in life the difference between the life you're living now and the life you want to live is having just a little more courage to take the steps toward creating the future you want. Anything is possible when you dare to go for your goals.

What keeps us from taking those steps?

Fear.

It manifests as this nagging, negative voice in our heads.

It is the killer of dreams. It keeps us from being brave. It keeps us from living our best life.

At times, this negative voice stops us from starting. Other times, it stops us from finishing. And at still other times, it stops us from sharing what we've completed.

It fills us with doubt. It tells us that we are not good enough. It tells us we're wasting our time. It tells us we are going to look foolish and fail.

It wants to keep us in a box. It wants to keep us small. It wants to keep us on the shore seeing sharks instead of dolphins.

For me, this negative voice has been there as long as I can remember. It greets me every morning when I sit down and write. It's there when I start any entrepreneurial venture. It's there whenever I want to step out of my comfort zone and try something new.

It fills me with excuses, procrastination, self-loathing, distraction, perfectionism—anything that keeps me from pursuing, let alone completing, my dreams and life's work.

After the heart attack, I made a few distinctions. I realized that this voice of negativity, this chattering mind, the fear, is always going to be there.

We all have it like we have a heartbeat.

I also recognized that my wonderful uniqueness and my life's work—the work I was put on earth to share—are on the other side of this negative voice. And for me to become the best expression of who I am meant to be, I must not only face the voice of negativity, but I must also defeat it every day.

My hopes.

My dreams.

My happiness depends on it.

This bears repeating. To overcome adversity, we must battle the negative voice, the doubt, the fear and insecurities every day.

Our hopes, dreams and happiness depend on it.

That means showing up each and every day and being brave and doing the work. It means pushing past all of your insecurities, your self-doubt, your procrastination habits, your perfectionism, and your fears.

The negative voice's target is our individuality, our genius, our soul, or incomparable gift that we were put on this earth to share.

Know this: the more fear you feel toward something, the more important it is to your soul's evolution.

For a long time I thought I had lost my passion. I wasn't feeling passion towards anything, nor could I identify the things I was willing to fight for. Things that got me out of bed feeling on fire and ready to take on the day.

There were many times when I felt lost and adrift. I chalked it up to not being in touch with my life's work, not knowing my life's purpose. I expected it all to unfold in front of me like some grand master plan or a movie.

Then it dawned on me that I hadn't lost my passion—*fear* had zapped the passion.

Fear of failure, fear of being broke, fear of going bankrupt, fear of being homeless, fear of what people would think if that happened, fear of criticism, of not following my life's work, and a multitude of other fears.

But if I was to boil it down to the biggest fear that nearly crushed me, it would be the fear of failure.

I wonder how many ventures are not started, how many dreams are not realized, how many lives are not changed by people simply never beginning or quitting before they reach the finish line because they—like me—were afraid to fail?

But remember, the fear, this negative voice, will always be there.

To cultivate happiness and live your best life you *must* continue on in spite of the fear.

This is *courage.*

It is a key principle of cultivating happiness and really living.

Too often though, we equate courage *only* with great, heroic acts. The firefighter rushing back into the burning building to save a person, or the innocent bystanders taking on the knife-wielding assailant. These are courageous and heroic acts of great sacrifice and should be celebrated.

But let us not forget the small acts of bravery that are performed each day.

One of the scariest things in life is to do what we actually want to do.

Sometimes it takes 100% of your strength and courage to just get out of bed and take on the day, to walk through the door of any new endeavor, to say "hi" to someone we find attractive, to ask for a raise, to say "no" to friends because we really want time to ourselves, to start before you are ready, to say... "I love you."

These moments, no matter how large or small, need to be celebrated. Nurture yourself. Show yourself generosity. You are worth it.

The time to be brave is now.

Each day is an opportunity to perform one small act of bravery.

Anything is possible when you have the courage to pursue your dreams.

What would you do in your life if you had just 10% more courage?

Don't let the fear of looking bad hold you back from doing something great and living the life of your dreams. Have courage in your heart. Face your fears each and every day.

Everything you want in life is right there in front of you.

All you have to do is reach out and grab it.

Happiness awaits.

Chapter 19: The Secret About Love

When life gets hard, we may want to give up.

You may have felt that way. I've felt that way too. But here is a secret that has gotten me through the many hard times since the heart attack. It's gotten me through times when I was feeling down, empty, lonely, and sad.

The secret is simple, but powerful.

Yet, I have to admit, I'm a little self-conscious about sharing this one. My jock friends will say I've gone soft, but I like to think of it as going tender in the heart.

When I'm feeling unlovable, like life is in a bad way, I sit quietly, legs crossed, hands resting in my lap, I breathe and…

I think about the people I love.

One by one I picture their faces and imagine them sitting directly across from me. I slowly breathe and let the love I feel for the person begin to build up and expand inside of me until it fills my existence.

I see the loving energy as a warm, golden light that radiates from my core and envelops my entire being.

I visualize this loving energy flowing gently outward from me to the other person. I imagine it filling every cell of their body until they too are glowing in this loving energy and we are connected by it.

In my mind, I tell them I love them. I see them nod and acknowledge my words. We then bask in the loving energy and connection.

Each and every time I do this I'm instantly reunited with the feeling of love.

I do this with my son.

My mother.

My brothers and sisters.

My nieces and nephews.

My significant other.

My friends.

My pups.

The way back to love begins by giving love. When we give love, it expands and multiplies. This is not egotistic love. It's love without condition. Love without boundaries. It exists in all races, all classes, all sexualities, all human beings. It connects, unites, and binds us all together.

It's the same love I saw, the love that connects us all, when I was wheeled into the emergency room during the heart attack and was floating above my body looking down at everyone below me.

I wasn't aware this type of love existed until the incident, and then I thought it was a one-shot deal. I had no idea that I could summon this love whenever I wanted.

In the past, love and happiness were tied to gratification and pleasing the senses. Temporary feelings that I felt when I got the girl, won the prize, bought the new car. The problem was these feelings were short-lived. No matter how hard I tried, I couldn't hold onto the feelings of gratification. The tighter I squeezed, the more the feeling slipped through my fingers.

I was chasing after a transitory feeling instead of connecting to the love that was already inside of me.

When you realize you already have the love you seek, and the ability to cultivate it, your life changes in amazing ways. It shifts your focus from lack and wanting to deep satisfaction, contentment, and peace.

The key is that you cannot feel this love with your mind.

You must use your *heart.*

By giving from the heart and expecting nothing in return, you connect to a loving source of energy beyond our intellectual understanding. When you are in harmony with this loving energy, life becomes a happy dream and there will never be a scarcity of love.

Each day you can open the door to this love by practicing loving connections.

Don't over-think this practice. Just do it.

Here is how you do it.

Sit comfortably in a chair or cross-legged on the floor in a place you won't be disturbed. Let your hands relax on your legs. Close your eyes. Take a few slow, gentle breaths and turn your focus inward.

Think about someone you love. Let an image of them float into your mind. It doesn't matter if it's in focus or not. Let the feelings of love you feel for this person fill your heart.

Breathe slowly and deeply. In your mind's eye, see the love as a luminescent glow that flows through you and surrounds your being. Be gentle with yourself. You'll know you've got it when you feel warmth and bliss fill your existence.

Now imagine this loving energy flowing from within you to the person. See it fill every cell of their body until they too are glowing in this loving energy and you are connected by it.

In your mind say, "I love you" to the person and see even more love flow from you to them. Imagine them receiving the love and saying, "thank you."

Sit for a moment and bask in the gentle embrace of love. Take a moment to acknowledge the depth of this love. The beauty. The bliss. The contentment. The happiness.

Stay in the flow of loving energy for as long as you'd like.

If you want to send love to another person, picture them in your mind, say "I love you" and send them love. See your love as an endless reservoir. The more love you send, the more love you feel, the more love you have to give.

When you're ready, say "thank you" to the universe and gently open your eyes and come back to the room.

The mind might wander during this practice. That's its nature. Each time it does, gently shift your focus back to sending and feeling love. I've had the best results doing this toward the end of my meditation sessions when my mind is already calm and my focus is deep.

Until I started this practice it never occurred to me how much love I could experience in my life and how much love I have in my heart.

This love fills me. It gives me a sense of contentment and a profound joy that I didn't know was possible. It's as if a door was suddenly opened to a deeper source of happiness and fulfillment than I'd previously known.

This love is also available to you at all times.

Try this practice and over time you will experience a sense of being filled with a happiness that is endless and complete.

You will never feel the lack of love again in your life.

Chapter 20: The Thief of Joy

I've got this buddy who makes a gazillion dollars a year. I'm not kidding. He is one of the highest paid execs in America. One year he made over 90 million dollars. He's got what everyone would think is an amazing life. A beautiful wife, great kids, houses on every coast, a private jet to whisk him around the country. He takes amazing, breathtaking trips around the world. He's also a genuinely good guy.

Whenever I compare myself to him, I can't help but feel like a failure. I'd love to make 90 million dollars a year—and am open to it—however, I'm not sure it's in the cards for me.

But I also know I'm not a failure. I know I've done, and will continue to do, things of value in my life.

It got me thinking about how we grade ourselves, and if we get the criteria correct, could it help us cultivate happiness?

I've never had the conversation with my buddy, but I'd guess that he grades himself on how many deals he makes and how much profit he can drive to his company.

When I grade myself on the same criteria, I feel like a failure. No one likes to feel like a failure. It's one of the most miserable feelings in the world. To have failed is human. To feel like a failure is something completely different.

That's when I realized that a tool for cultivating happiness is to know what's important to each of us and how to grade ourselves by that measure.

For some people, it's about how much money they make.

For others, it's about how much money they give away.

For some, it's about being in service. For example, when Mother Teresa won the Nobel Peace Prize, she asked that the $192,000 prize be given to the poor in India.

For others, it's about the number of people who serve them.

For some people, it's about effecting world change.

For others, it's mentoring a few.

For me, personally, it has become about connecting with others and learning to find happiness, love, and joy within myself so I can be an expression of this, and to help people to live a happier, healthier, more inspired life.

When I'm walking down this path, focused on these values, is when I'm happiest.

Conversely, when I compare myself to others, when I'm only acquiring things and get lost in personal achievement, it doesn't make me happy. I've been down the "it's all about me road" and it wasn't joyful, because it was never enough.

It only matters when I can live in accordance with my values.

It only matters when I can create, motivate and inspire.

Celebrate your unique gifts and achievements.

Live your own life based upon your own values. Live it fully.

Don't compare your life to others.

Comparison is the thief of joy.

Chapter 21: It's Not Always About You

It shouldn't have been about me.

But I forgot something vital in that moment.

It happened last December when I had the opportunity to be the keynote speaker at the *Overcoming Adversity* conference in one of my favorite cities, San Antonio, Texas.

When I speak at an event my mission is to be an agent of change and to motivate people to live a radically inspired life. It's important for me to connect with each and every member of the audience and make an impact on their lives in a positive way.

I take this mission quite seriously. I realize that being able to speak, to have people's attention, is an honor and I want to make sure I deliver something of value.

The conference took place in a quaint, intimate environment. The event, not unlike a lot of other events, is running behind schedule. By the time I hit the stage, it's already 10:30 p.m. I'm concerned the audience is exhausted and ready to head home.

After a few minutes on stage, however, my worries subside. I'm really connecting with the audience. More than connecting, I'm slaying it. There is a collective silence as I speak. Everyone is with me. I feel pumped up and invigorated, like this is exactly where I am supposed to be.

I move back and forth across the stage sharing my story, reveling in how good it feels to have everyone with me, when I spot this this big, lumbering early 20-something guy, sitting smack in the middle of the front row.

He is so not with me.

He's falling asleep.

I can't help but notice the woman sitting next to him, nudging him, trying to keep him awake.

I have to be honest. This irritates and pisses me off.

I know it comes with the territory, and the focus should be on the people who I can help and those who need to hear the message. I remind myself of my motto: *If I can help just one person—it's a good day.*

I keep rolling with my speech, but I can't help coming back to the sleeping guy in the middle of the front row.

No matter where I look I see him.

I'm angry at this guy's lack of respect. I'm also angry with myself for being so petty, but the longer I speak, the more disdain I feel for this guy.

If you have ever wondered if speakers or performers can see you when you're not paying attention and are talking, texting or sleeping, be assured—WE CAN.

I plow onward with the speech and deliver the message to those who were open and ready to hear it. I know I impacted a lot of people, and all in all it was an amazing night.

After the speech, there is a meet and greet with the audience. I'm definitely a people person and love meeting people face to face. I gratefully shake hands, answer questions and thank people for coming. A person approaches with a copy of my first book *Gladiator*. I humbly sign it and thank them for coming.

When I look up, the *sleeper* is now standing in front of me with two other adults. I can feel my stomach tighten, but I smile at him because I'm evolved. Truthfully, I smile at him because that's just what you do at events like this. But behind my smile I still feel contempt for him.

The woman accompanying him is the same woman who had kept nudging him awake. She tells me how much she enjoyed the speech and how she needed to hear it. She told me she understood *adversity*.

I nod, smile and thank her for coming. She then introduces me to the *sleeper*.

"This is my son," she says. "He's 22 and he's *autistic*."

The words hang in the air. I am stunned.

She then motions to her son holding out a comic book of "Marvel Super Heroes" and continues, "My son used to watch you on TV. He thinks you're a superhero, too, and wants you to sign his comic book."

I look at her, unable to speak. I feel an unendurable assault of emotions rise in me, and in an instant I'm ashamed and humbled.

She says, "He never stays up this late but refused to leave until after he got to meet you and you signed his book."

I suck in a stiff breath and look closely at this young man, at this beautiful soul, at his light shining bright as he holds out his comic book.

I take his book and sign it while he patiently waits. I can see this is a big thing for him. When I hand him back his book, he suddenly wraps me up in a big two-arm hug and squeezes me for all he was worth and says, "Thank you."

His parents look astonished.

They tell me he never hugs anyone, and that showed how special I was to him. It takes everything I have to not start weeping.

As they walk off into the crowd, I stare after them for a long moment and realize the *biggest lesson* of the night was taught by this special young man.

Sometimes guides and teachers come to us in the most *unexpected* ways.

Sometimes what we see isn't an accurate reflection of reality.

Sometimes we need to change our lens, our perspective, to see clearly.

I made the mistake of believing my first impression and made the situation about me. I made tonight about me. It should never be about me. I interpreted his actions as something he did to belittle me.

When the truth is, this young man's actions were HEROIC.

He stayed up late. He went to a conference. He pushed past his comfort zone and hugged a complete stranger.

I learned a valuable lesson that night about looking past first impressions and giving people the benefit of the doubt. They might be having a bad day. They might have lost their job, have gotten divorced, found out they or a loved one has cancer.

Don't always trust your first impression. Your lens may be out of focus. Take some time to investigate and look beyond your gut reaction and see the human being standing in front of you. Then dig even deeper and try and see the light in each human being that connects us all.

When we open our hearts and see things differently, events and their meanings can change in an instant.

Chapter 22: The Value of Valuing Others

My friend Michael does the coolest thing every time we go out to dinner. He takes the time to introduce himself and his wife to the server and he learns their name as well—and makes sure to address the server by their name throughout dinner.

Every time Michael does this, I see the surprise and delight on the server's face. More than one waiter/waitress has thanked him. This simple habit only takes 30 seconds, but it speaks volumes about a person and their respect for others.

The server-customer relationship is one of the last places where we get to clearly see the nature of class and privilege play out. I've seen too many people who don't even look at the server when they order. They simply grunt and point at the menu while they're talking on the phone.

They don't see the *human being* standing in front of them.

People want to be seen. People want connection. People want to feel valued. When we treat people as objects, we degrade them. We're telling them they're invisible, and of no value to us.

If you ever wonder why customer service has gone to hell, just take a look at the way you or people you dine with treat your server, or a supermarket checker, or for that matter, anyone in the service industry. Common courtesy is never out of place.

A few years back, following Michael's lead, I began introducing myself to the server and asking their name, and wow did my service change.

I remember one night in particular. I was eating at a small diner that was abnormally busy. The service was slow. One waitress was stuck with the task of trying to cover the entire restaurant by herself. I could see that she was rushed and flustered.

When she came to take my order, I introduced myself, and my dining companion, and asked her name. This must have caught her by surprise because she took a deep breath, then tears welled up in her eyes and she said, "Thank you for asking. Nobody ever asks. It's like...they don't even think of me as a person."

More tears fell as she said, "Thank you. Thank you so much."

I don't know what it feels like to be her, but I do know what it feels like to be disrespected and not seen. I think we all experience that at different times during our lives, and yet while we hate the feeling, we are the first to do the same to someone else, even if unintentionally.

Treat people like human beings and see the humanity in each person regardless of their station in life. We are spiritual beings having a human experience. The moment you recognize this—your life changes.

If you want better service, try taking a moment to introduce yourself to the person waiting on you. I promise you, it will make all the difference.

Chapter 23: Forgiveness

I sit by his bed side.

He was a dear friend.

His life force is weak. It's hard for me to see him like this. But I had to see him.

He will die soon. Cancer is getting the best of him now.

I sit for 10 minutes. 15 minutes. Finally, his eyes blink open and slowly focus on me. It takes all of his energy to smile. To speak.

"Thank you for coming," he whispers in a raspy, dry voice.

I smile, reach out and take his hand in mine. I never thought I'd be holding this man's hand. Not in a million years.

He and I went through countless battles on the football field. We fought together. We smacked each other on the shoulder pads and bumped chests. We hooted and hollered.

But that was back then. Back when we were warriors.

Now, I'm holding his hand.

Gently.

Tenderly.

We are two human beings sharing a moment of human truth. The truth is I love this man. I love him like a brother. Death breaks down barriers.

I ask him if others have come.

He says, "A few."

He blinks, swallows hard, fights back some kind of unseen pain. As he focuses back on me, tears well up in his eyes as he speaks.

“But you...” He stops mid-sentence. “I didn’t think... you’d come.”

There was a time when we were the best of friends. Then we had a falling out. Our egos, our pride and anger took over. Harsh words were spoken. There was the threat of a fight.

A friendship was lost.

But not forgotten.

More tears fall as he struggles to speak. His words grow heavy with regret. “I’m sorry... I didn’t come when...you...” He is weeping now. “...when you had your...heart attack.”

I squeeze his hand firmly and let him know it’s okay. I find a small cloth and wipe away his tears. This was the same man who tore guys apart with his hands on the football field. Now he is too weak to tend to his own tears.

We sit. Say nothing. He takes labored breaths. After a long moment his eyes find mine again.

“I’m going to die...” he says with an inevitability tinged with sadness.

The emotion wells up in me. I nod that I know.

“I’m sorry… for what happened,” he says.

I nod in agreement, but the truth is I can’t remember exactly what the falling out was about. It may have been a culmination of things: girls, a business deal, a slight that led to the near fight.

But back then it was easier to be angry. The size of our egos wouldn’t let us back down or say we were sorry. We were drunk on youth, swagger and bravado.

My friend continues, “The bitterness… the grudges… makes my heart heavy.” He pauses, takes another labored breath. “I want to get rid of it… before… I go.”

I nod that I understand and clasp his hand in both of mine. “I got you man. I’m sorry too. We’re all good.”

His face suddenly relaxes. He squeezes my hand faintly and his breathing eases.

In that moment, I could feel the bitterness go away.

It is just…gone. And we are at peace.

He starts to speak again, but stops mid-sentence and drifts to sleep.

To my surprise, I find it comforting to be with him during this time, to sit by his side and hold his hand and watch his chest rise and fall. I know what it feels like to be close to death. I didn't want him to be alone.

After a few hours, I finally leave.

It was the last time I saw him.

He died the next day.

I'm happy we got to have that moment. Too many times people pass without getting to express their regrets or have a chance to resolve their conflicts and find peace.

The encounter also got me thinking about how much baggage we unnecessarily carry through our lives, and how we only wait until the end to drop it and resolve our conflicts.

We hold onto grudges for years and years. We feel self-righteous because of what *they* did to us and we become stuck in a prison of self-imposed resentment.

Yes, we get to be right by doing that. But it keeps us from truly being happy.

I too have held onto grudges for too long, and I have hard places in my heart where I've clung to anger and resentment. I feel the weight of the anger and pain now. I know the anger doesn't serve me. It keeps part of my heart dark and void of love.

I realize sometimes we hold on to anger to remind ourselves to not repeat the mistake that caused us the pain. Other times we cling to the anger because we don't have the tools to forgive.

But this I know for sure. Life is too short to have bitterness in our hearts. Plus, we can't have gratitude and true happiness in our lives without forgiveness.

But what is forgiveness and how do we forgive?

The trick doesn't lie in never having conflicts but in resolving them as soon as you can.

Forgiveness is a decision to move forward and let go of bitterness and ideas of revenge. Forgiving doesn't mean that you negate the other person's responsibility for hurting you, and it doesn't diminish or justify the wrong. You can forgive a person without excusing the act.

Forgiveness brings a peace that lets you go on with the rest of your life.

Sometimes, forgiveness is about letting go of the resentment you feel when thinking about the person who wronged you. It's embodying the idea that you can't change the past but you can choose to let it go.

When you let go, you allow yourself to be free.

You allow yourself to come out of the prison of anger and resentment and step into the sunshine of life. Don't waste time trying to get even. It doesn't work.

Drop the past and work on loving yourself now.

It's not easy. To forgive, your heart must be generous. It's so hard because the goodness and love in your heart have to penetrate resentment, hate, ego, fear and frustration. But by letting go of grudges and bitterness you make way for happiness, health and peace in your life.

You have a choice. You can either fight for love and happiness and have an open heart, or you can let the anger and resentment destroy everything.

When you do forgive and continue to work at being a good and loving person, it sends the personal message that love is stronger than hate or fear.

Don't wait until the end to resolve your conflicts and find peace. Make the decision to put the baggage down. Start now and set yourself free. You'll be astonished at the lightness, freedom and love you will feel in your heart.

Chapter 24: Love and Relationships

I couldn't pretend like everything was okay, because it wasn't.

At the same time things weren't bad. There had been love and laughter. She had been my best friend, my confidant, and my support system.

I'd been with her nearly twelve years. Almost a quarter of my life.

I didn't have the words to express how I was feeling, and even if I had, I don't think I had the courage to say them. But I knew I had to open up about my feelings in order to start the process toward authenticity. To honor her. To honor myself.

Through the experience of the heart attack, I recognized more than ever, that even with great love it's hard to get all the pieces to fall in place and sometimes it doesn't work out.

Yet I usually had an answer, some kind of answer, to any sort of problem. But for this moment, this problem, I had no answers. All I had to go on was what I felt in my heart. And in my heart, I knew that walking down the romantic path together was not going to be our life-long destiny.

The realization was devastating.

There was never going to be a good time. It wasn't going to be easy.

Choking back the tears, sitting in the living room of our home, on the couch we purchased together, I decided, after months of discussion and deep introspection, to end the romantic leg of our journey.

We sat there for a long time after the conversation. Saying nothing. The distance between people can be staggering. She was only a few feet from me but felt miles away. My eyes drifted across the living room furniture, the walls, the shelves, all crowded with memories of our life together, until they came back and found her.

I can still see her face.

The shock.

The tears.

The pain.

Caused by me.

I felt selfish and ungrateful. Like a bad man. I was stabbing my best friend and partner in the back after so many years of being together. My grief was palpable. I felt an intense loneliness. I was losing one of my closest companions.

Yet, I knew it was the right thing to do. I loved her enough to let her go because I wanted her to be happy, and I realized that we just weren't capable of being happy together.

To be honest, I'm not sure if this is true. Maybe we were happy, but it was just that the "best-friendedness" had taken over and the intimacy had slowly faded. I'm not sure when, exactly, the intimacy left the relationship. It's more like we gradually became the best of friends, and even though I valued and cherished our friendship, history, and life together, I wanted more from the romantic relationship in my life.

Some may see a relationship that didn't end with "till death do us part" as a failure.

They couldn't be more wrong. There was a tremendous amount of support and caring and trust. We lived, loved, and laughed. We had too many good memories and amazing times to ever say we had a bad relationship. And I certainly wasn't out searching for someone else to make me happy. I wouldn't put that pressure on anyone. I know now, more than ever, that the amount of happiness I experience in my life is up to me and I take full ownership of that.

I also take responsibility for our relationship if I wasn't able to meet her expectations and be the man she wanted me to be. Or if I wasn't there enough, or if she didn't feel loved and supported and cared for enough. For that, I am truly sorry.

Yet even with these words and thoughts, I still couldn't find a way to part in beauty and grace when we both had broken hearts. There was anger, resentment, grief, and bitterness. We thought we'd be together forever.

Then I read something that changed everything.

It was the idea of conscious uncoupling.

Author Katherine Woodward Thomas described conscious uncoupling as "*a break up or divorce that is characterized by a tremendous amount of goodwill, generosity, and respect, where those separating strive to do minimal damage to each other and their children if they have them...*"

In her book *Conscious Uncoupling*, Thomas goes on to say, "*Conscious Uncouplings are most known for their bountiful acts of kindness, bighearted gestures of goodness, and genuine efforts to do the right thing for the right reason.*"

This made sense to me. It felt like a better way than to simply separate. A way that was more in tune with who I was as a person. That last thing I wanted to do was leave the relationship in a way that would damage all the wonderful times and love we shared.

It hasn't been easy. It's taken all I had. It's taken deep soul-searching, prayer, and meditation to find a way to handle the break-up with generosity, goodness, and kindness that celebrated and respected our time together.

My ego and pride still get in the way. There is wreckage unresolved and hearts that have not healed. But whenever I feel the anger or urge to win and be right or act out in some mean-spirited way, I tell myself to breathe and relax and remember my intention to uncouple with kindness and love.

My respect and the value I hold for what we had is much greater than a kitchen table, a piece of artwork, or any other material possession we owned. I am comforted because I know the pain will be gone soon but the wisdom I've gained will remain.

My hope is that she will read this and know that I still love her and care about her, and that I'm sorry.

I'm sorry you are hurting.

I'm sorry I've caused you pain.

I can promise I did my best for the man I was at the time.

I am a work in progress. I am flawed. Yet, I am forever blossoming into the man that I want to be.

I'll always care about you.

I miss you.

I miss our friendship.

Endings are never easy.

But they don't have to be bad.

Sometimes the hardest conversations are often the most important ones to have.

I've learned that time doesn't make things right. We must actively work to make things right.

If your relationship is broken, make every attempt to breathe life into it. Trust, friendship, history, and family have tremendous value in the overall meaning of things. Take responsibility for your feelings and move from blaming your partner to looking inside of yourself with genuine honesty and reflection. Often, when we do this we find old wounds from past relationships that affect the way we see our partners.

Too often we anoint our partners as the *special person* who is going to finally make us happy and we put an unrealistic expectation on them to fulfill the role of the happiness provider in our lives.

It isn't until we learn to take responsibility for cultivating our own happiness that we can truly be free to experience unconditional and empowering love.

I believe that happiness in a relationship occurs when you each live your own life and go down your own path, but along the journey you build bridges across to each other where you meet.

This is the intersection between love and personal enlightenment.

Now, if you've tried with everything you have and your relationship still isn't working, and you decide to separate, then please honor your time together and the love you have for each other by moving through the transition in your relationship with integrity, grace, honor, and respect.

I'm aware that, unfortunately, your partner may not see your relationship the same way. But you can't control how they are going to react. You can only control how you respond and make a commitment to stay true to your intention. You can only do everything and all you can; after that, you have to surrender to the moment and let go of your attachments to how you want things to be and accept them as they are.

This doesn't mean changing who you are or not standing up for what is rightly yours. It means always keeping true to your higher self and how you want to be in the world—because what you are is so magnificent that it far exceeds your wildest imagination and dreams.

It may take a little time to wade through the forest of hurt and pain to see the magnificence of who you are, but I promise you it is there.

Work on cultivating your own happiness and living a life full of gratitude, appreciation and joy to see the beauty of who you are.

I also realize that often we don't leave relationships out of fear of being alone. Fear that no one else will want us. If this is you, your mission right now is to love yourself in the ways you need to be loved, standing strong in the truth of your own value and worthiness to be loved, no matter what.

If your relationship is working and you are happy, love the person you are with, with all you've got. Make the choice to be happy and build bridges to each other rather than throwing up the roadblocks of always having to be right. Don't waste time on things that don't matter with the people who matter.

There is no better time to take a stand for your life than this moment.

My wish is that you live happily ever after or live happily *even* after.

Chapter 25: Broken, Yet More Beautiful

"The world breaks everyone and afterward many are strong at the broken places."

~Hemingway

There is a belief in western culture that broken things have lost their value, and they are often discarded or thrown away.

Kintsugi is the centuries-old Japanese art of repairing pottery with gold or silver lacquer. When kintsugi is used to mend together broken pottery, the cracks are highlighted, rather than hidden, turning the object into something that is one of a kind and uniquely exquisite, something that is often more valuable than the original.

The belief is that when something is damaged and has a history, it becomes more beautiful.

During the course of our lives many of us will have something tragic happen suddenly. No amount of experience can prepare us for the moment.

A cancer diagnosis.

An accident that steals away a loved one.

A sick child.

Divorce.

A business deal that goes bad.

A heart attack.

Regardless of the cause, everything will change in an instant.

In a world that's suddenly turned upside-down, there is one thing I know with rock-solid certainty. That moment gives you a chance to either rise up and become strong at the place you were broken or fall back in despair and hopelessness.

What you choose will determine the life you live.

You have the choice to be angry for everything you lost or be grateful for everything you *do* have. You have the choice to see what you can be in spite of your circumstances. You have the choice to change an obstacle into an opportunity.

Or, on a deeper level, you have the choice to change a tragedy and heartache into a gift of inspiration for others.

It's difficult to find strength in the face of adversity. Recovering from a life-shattering experience might be the most difficult thing in the world. No one knows what it's like to be you and what you've gone through. Yet, there is comfort in the shared experience.

As human beings, I believe, we have all been broken or damaged in some way. We all hit hard times. We all struggle. We all fall down, and many times we don't feel like we have the strength to get back up or that we will ever feel joy again.

But the human spirit has an amazing capacity to persevere. For every setback there is a chance to come back. But it's more than just about coming back, it's about coming back transformed. Your mission is to rise up and become strong at the places where you are broken.

It starts with knowing you are beautiful the way you are.

You are special.

You are loved.

Use these words to find the courage to see the possibilities in front of you right now.

Your goal may seem distant and unattainable. I remember feeling that way too after the heart attack, when I was standing at the top of the stairs, and my goal for the entire day was to walk down the stairs, touch the refrigerator and not die. I never dreamed of not only coming back, but coming back damaged and being more beautiful because of it.

It's hard for me to write those words. It's hard to accept and love what is damaged within ourselves. It's even harder to tell ourselves we are beautiful.

For a long time I thought life would never be good again. I thought my best days where behind me. I wasn't sure I'd ever be happy again. It's easy to get overwhelmed, lose belief and give into our circumstances and quit. But to stand back up and repair what is broken, you have to believe in something you cannot see.

This is called *faith.*

Each day you have to put one foot in front of the other and do just a little better, and have faith that it's possible to grow, and find deeper meaning and appreciation in our lives even after the most devastating events.

It happened after my brother died in my arms.

It happened again after the heart attack.

No matter what your setback is, no matter where or how you are damaged, there is the opportunity to become strong where we are broken and rediscover joy.

It's time to be proudly imperfect.

It's time to embrace your healing and find gold in your scars.

You are beautiful.
You are special.
You are loved.

Chapter 26: All We Can Do Is *Everything* We Can Do

As we age it gets harder to bounce back quickly.

It happens with the body. It also happens with the spirit, making it harder to find the will and courage to start again after something doesn't turn out the way we thought it would.

We can work really hard at something and have it not turn out the way we want it to. It's happened quite a few times in my life.

One vivid example of this happened after I starred on the *American Gladiators* for seven years. I got a three-picture deal from Warner Brothers to be the next big action star. They bought a script with me in mind as the lead, hired a director, and were paying me $50,000 every three months on a holding deal.

I thought for sure the movie would be made and my life would be a Hollywood dream. After a year, the checks stopped coming and my calls weren't returned.

It—disappointment—happened again later after I sold my first screenplay. I thought the work would roll in and everything would be easier. It wasn't. Screenwriting jobs were just as hard to get as before, but it was much more disappointing not getting them because my expectations had changed.

It happened after I directed my first and only independent movie. I didn't get the response I wanted, even though we sold the movie and made the investors all their money back. That's a big win in Hollywood.

The idea of getting a three-picture deal, selling scripts, directing and selling a movie are all huge accomplishments when I look back on them. But at the time, they all felt like disappointments because I didn't get the results I had hoped for.

And each time, it got harder to hide the crushing disappointment and bounce back.

It happened again after I wrote my first book and had it published by one of the biggest publishers in the world. Just having a book published by a renowned publisher should have been a celebrated feat.

But again, when it didn't hit the *New York Times* bestseller list, I was disappointed. In fact, as you know, I quit writing for six years.

I couldn't bounce back.

Maybe I dream too big. But I believe in living a big life.

After the heart attack, I vowed not to waste energy on things I couldn't influence. I couldn't make the ambulance go any faster on the way to the hospital; I couldn't help the paramedics resuscitate me; I couldn't help the cardiologist with my surgery.

What I could do was take all the energy I had and channel it into learning everything I could about why people have heart attacks, what people who survive do, and what I could do to give myself the best chance of survival.

The results were out of my control. Whether I survived or not was out of my control.

That's when I realized *all we can do is what we can do.*

I don't worry about or try to control my survival. I do the best and all I can do.

I've learned to apply this same philosophy to my work.

To let go of the attachment. To not let perfect be the enemy of done.

I admit, it's a constant battle.

When we are ambitious and care about our career and legacy, it's natural to put our head down and work hard to do everything possible to be successful. But when the work is finally out there, when we've done the best we can, that's when we have to let go of our attachment to the results.

The challenge is making peace with the results because they don't always happen the way we think they should.

It's like the writing of this book. I hope that it will inspire millions, make the bestseller lists, and change people's lives. But the truth is, I have very little control over what happens after I finish it. I can work hard and write the best book possible. I can hire a publicist and do everything imaginable to promote the book, but at the end of the day I have almost no control over the marketplace.

When we put things into the world without attachment, we give them their own life.

We can simply do the best we can do. And realize, all we can do is everything we can do.

If things don't go as I hope, the goal is to make sure the results don't deter me from bouncing back. I know this might sound a bit simplistic. But coming to terms with what I can influence and what I cannot has given me the courage to write again.

This book comes from that belief.

If this book doesn't go the way I want it to, all I need is a little courage and grit to start again. I believe I have it in me. The question is, do you?

Is there something in your life that you've abandoned because you didn't have the strength to start again?

Is there a hidden project you've been dreaming about doing but were afraid to begin because of what others might think, or because you were too concerned about the outcome?

I cannot tell you how many times I've heard someone say they wish they had more time to pursue their dreams. The problem is we think we have time. We put off things until "someday," and that leads to never. Regret is a heartbreaking emotion and we often don't see it until we are near the end.

Don't wait.

Start today.

Do all you can do. Breathe life into your dream. Let your life shine bright.

The world is waiting for your gifts, your artistry, your voice, your beauty.

You got this.

I believe in you.

Chapter 27: In the End It's Simple

When I was lying in the hospital the morning after the heart attack and I wasn't sure if I was going to make it, I didn't think about how many homes or cars I had. I didn't think about the money I'd earned, my achievements, or about the number of trophies or plaques I had on the wall.

I only thought about one thing.

The people I loved and how I wanted them near me.

In the end, it was that simple.

I wanted the people I loved close to me. And I wanted the people I loved to know how much I cared about them.

Facing your mortality shines a light on what you love in life, your reasons to live, and how you want to live. In that instant, everything changed and I realized what is important in life.

Family.

Love.

Gratitude and appreciation.

Being in service.

Pursuing the dreams deep in your heart.

Making the choice to live fully and be happy now.

Since the heart attack, I don't postpone things in life. I don't say someday. I know time isn't guaranteed.

I don't strive to live a perfect life. I strive to live a happy life.

I've become a collector of moments instead of things. I try to mend any broken fences, because I know having regrets in the end is a painful thing. I've also come to realize that it's often not our extraordinary actions that make a difference, but the small things we do for others with extraordinary love.

I believe in working hard, staying humble, being kind and living a life full of service, purpose and gratitude—and perhaps most importantly of all—I believe in spending time with people I love and care about.

This includes my son, my beautiful boy. He's a young man now, strong and handsome. Whenever I see him, I lap up and luxuriate in every drop of his smile and tell myself to remember the moment. They are precious and fleeting and gone in the blink of an eye.

I also realized working on the weekend to finish a chapter or to get a deal done isn't all that vital. That it's more important to visit my mother, catch one of my nieces' or nephews' soccer games, or meet my son for lunch. I've learned it's not so crucial to have the last word in an argument with someone I care about—to not waste time on things that don't matter with the people that do matter.

I've discovered that I'm attracted to peace and solitude and nature more than being in the middle of the action. I'm also more at ease in my own skin. I no longer have to have a drink in social situations to make myself feel more comfortable. I don't care as much about what people think about me. I know that I'm a good man and a kind human being.

I'm happier. I smile more. I'm less judgmental and give people the benefit of the doubt. I'm more thoughtful and considerate. I don't sweat the small stuff. I've found that lifting people up and helping them shine makes me happy.

Some days I have more to give than others, but each day, I make it a vow to give in whatever way I can, to whoever it is that needs it, even if it's just an encouraging word.

I no longer chase happiness, because I know exactly where to find it.

It is in me. Just as it is inside of you.

There are times that I still struggle. Times when it's hard to see the sunshine through the dusty window of my soul. Times when thoughts of the heart attack float to the surface and I feel the anger rise inside of me.

That's when I remind myself to breathe, to look at all the miracles of life happening all around me, and remind myself that it's hard to be angry when there is so much beauty in the world.

I focus on the beauty and my pain flies away.

My wish for you is... that you live a happy and bountiful life with days full of grace and beauty. That each day you discover inner peace and serenity, and have the courage to follow the dreams deep in your heart, and step boldly into your happiness and fully live.

The most important thing you need to know is that happiness *is* available to you at all times.

All you need to do is to cultivate it, and in very short order, with very little effort everything will fall into place.

Yes, it is work.

But it's not hard work.

It's work that when done over time will make an incredible and profound impact on your life and those around you.

Here is the best part, one that makes me smile as I write this. You think you need to feel confident or courageous in order to get started cultivating happiness? You don't. You just need to start.

If you can accept the fact that you may never feel ready, yet you can still push yourself forward, happiness will abound.

Have faith.

Follow through.

Walk with an open heart and be completely ready for whatever may come. You are a beautiful, unique being, worthy of love and acceptance, and have greatness in you. Let this book be the spark that ignites a fire in you to live better, be happier and appreciate every moment of your life.

Remember, happiness is a choice.

Choose happiness.

Start to cultivate it today.

You are worth it.

Share

I wrote this book from the heart. To share what I've learned, to share something that has been beautiful and life-changing for me.

I was a little scared to share this book. It's personal.

It shows me in a different light—vulnerable.

But I also believe the best thing we can share with others is our happiness.

If you liked what I've shared, please share it with friends.

It'll make them happy.

APPENDIX: INSTRUCTIONS

GRATITUDE: COLLECTING SMALL MOMENTS OF JOY

The first step in practicing gratitude is to make the choice to recognize the small, happy moments in life: the little things, the ordinary moments that might have slipped by you in the past.

Think of the sun breaking through the clouds on a rainy day, your child's laughter, hitting all the green lights, getting a good night's sleep, an unexpected smile from a stranger.

These gems are often hiding in plain sight. We only need to shine a little light on them and acknowledge them.

When you come across one of these moments, take a beat and let yourself feel the gratitude and exquisiteness of this simple happening.

I like to take a breath in when I spot one of these moments as a way to embrace and remember the moment. Then on the exhale, I'll say "thank you" to myself to express my gratitude.

For example, I'll be walking from my car into Starbucks and notice that it's a nice sunny day and the sun feels good on my face. I'll take a quick second to acknowledge the moment.

On the inhale, I'll say to myself, "The sun feels good on my face."

On the exhale I'll say, "Thank you."

When we acknowledge and pay attention to the positive moments, we are becoming active architects of our own happiness. This simple practice takes seconds to do and starts to fill our reservoir with little moments of joy that in turn create a wellspring of happiness that flows to all parts of our lives.

Another way to think about it is—every time you acknowledge a simple, happy moment you are making a deposit in your happiness bank. Do this often and "KA-CHING!" your bank account becomes full, and you're rich with happiness.

If you didn't create your list of small moments of happiness when you read Chapter 4: There is Happiness Everywhere, take 5-10 minutes now to make your list and start your collection.

By creating a list you are acknowledging the moments that already exist in your life, and are training yourself to see more of them.

What we focus on in life grows.

Start a habit now of shining a light on these little moments and watch the gratitude pour in. This daily practice has made a tremendous change in my life. It's made me happier. I no longer wait for the big moments to feel happy. I find and feel happy several times each and every day.

Here are the steps.

> Step 1. Make the choice to turn your radar on and start to look for these small, daily moments of happiness. They are happening all around you—you only need to teach yourself to see them.

Step 2. When you spot one of these moments, take a second to acknowledge it with a deep breath in. During the inhale say to yourself exactly what is wonderful about the moment. For instance: I love the sound of my child's laughter, these flowers are beautiful, I love the smell of coffee in the morning, the sun feels good on my face, I'm grateful for my partner, watching those puppies play is heartwarming.

Step 3. After you've acknowledged the moment, exhale and express your gratitude for the moment by saying to yourself, "Thank you." When we give thanks and express our gratitude we are also cultivating appreciation. Together they are the gateway to happiness.

Remember the frequency of your positive experiences is a much better forecaster of your happiness than the magnitude of your positive experiences.

This exercise only takes *10 seconds.*

I recommend doing it at least three times throughout the day. That's a total of 30 seconds. We can all find 30 seconds in our day to do this exercise. It's one of the best and most simple ways to bring more happiness into your life.

GRATITUDE: THE MORNING PRACTICE

Each day, shortly after I wake, I take out my gratitude journal and write down three things in my life that I'm grateful for. It only takes 2-3 minutes but sets the tone for the entire day.

Here is a sample from my Gratitude Journal.

<u>I am Grateful for...</u>

1. My health. Woohoo! I'm still alive and kicking.
2. How well my son is doing and how close we are.
3. My incredible family and friends.

No matter what your situation in life is, you can still find three things to be grateful for. It may be something as simple as being alive or having a roof over your head or having food on the table.

Every day won't be perfect, but by focusing on what we are grateful for, we bring incredible benefits into our lives.

Gratitude researchers Emmons and McCollough found in their landmark 2003 study that those who kept a daily gratitude journal on a regular basis felt better about their lives as a whole; exercised more regularly; slept better; felt higher levels of positivity, energy and enthusiasm; and had a greater sense of connectedness to others.

If these benefits sound good to you, start practicing them. If you want to take it to the next level, add the night gratitude practice.

GRATITUDE: THE NIGHT PRACTICE

In the evening, before I go to bed, I perform the second part of my daily gratitude practice by asking myself the simple question:

"What was great about today?"

I pick three moments from the day that I recognize as great. Again, it only takes 2-3 minutes. It's a way of taking inventory, then collecting and shining a light on the positive moments of the day.

I use the word "great" instead of "good" because the intensity of great is exponentially more powerful than good, and I'm only looking for awesomeness. Remember that what we focus on is what we create in our lives.

You want to live a great life. Look for great moments.

Here is a sample from my "What was great about today?" list.

What was Great about Today?

1. My son called me for no reason at all.
2. I finished writing a chapter in my new book.
3. Listened to an amazing Ted Talk.

When you write down these moments, focus on them and elevate them to "great," it's amazing the positive effect it has on your state of being. Too often the victories and what was great about the day get lost and forgotten in the busyness of life. When we take time to acknowledge them and write them down, we get the benefit and pleasure of experiencing them again.

Many times there will be an overlap between the items on your "There is Happiness Everywhere" list and "What is Great About Today" entries. That's okay—we can never have too many good things in our lives.

Start your gratitude practice now and watch happiness and joy beat a pathway to your door.

MEDITATION

A lot of people looking for happiness are told: "*True happiness isn't out there. It's within you.*" But they are not told where happiness is within them or how to find it.

For me, meditation has been the path to happiness and peace.

Below is a basic mindful meditation.

Here are the steps:

1. Set a timer so that you don't have to check your watch. There are apps for this or use your cell phone. I use my Apple watch. Start with 5 minutes.

2. Sit comfortably, but also sit with dignity, and keep your spine straight. I like to sit on a large pillow with my legs crossed and my hands gently resting on my lap in the mudra or Hokkaijoin position depicted below. I'm not a terribly flexible guy so I sit with my legs crossed and my lower back supported up against the sofa or a low profile bed. On days my knees are hurting, I'll sit in a chair with my spine straight and my hands in the same mudra position.

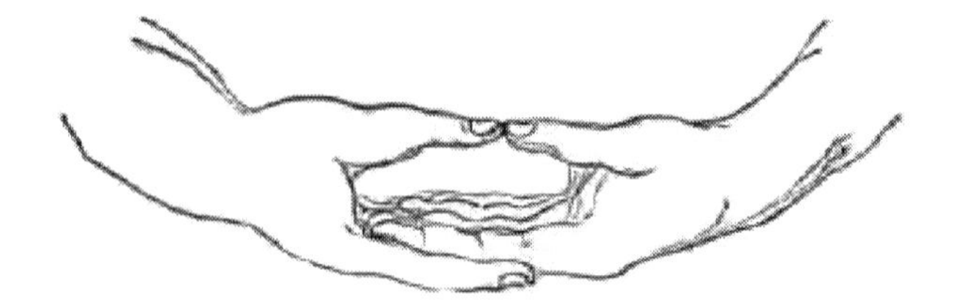

3. Being comfortable is important, but you don't want to relax too much and fall asleep. I generally keep my eyes open to prevent me from becoming drowsy. Without focusing on anything in particular, I direct my gaze to the floor about 2-3 feet in front of me. Eventually my eyes come to rest in a position that is half open and half closed.

4. Focus on your breath. Pick a spot and really try to feel the in-breath and the out-breath. I like focusing on the sensation of the incoming air as it moves past the outer portion of my nostrils and up in to the septum. I focus on this area for the inhale and the exhale.

5. Another trick to stay focused is to count your breaths. Start at one and work your

way up to ten. If you lose focus go back to one. If you get to ten also go back to one.

6. Your mind will wander during meditation. That's its nature. When it does, simply come back and focus on your breath or counting. Many people get frustrated by their wandering thoughts and inability to focus. What they don't realize is that the practice of catching the mind wandering and coming back to focus again and again, *is* the actual practice of meditation.

7. Trust and have faith in what you cannot see. The benefits of meditation may not be immediately felt, but over time and with consistent practice, it will have a profound impact on your life. For me, I discovered the peace, grace and tranquility that I had always sought.

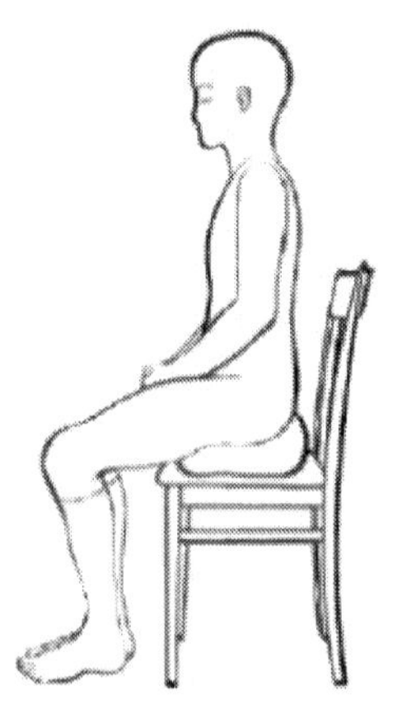

MORE TIPS ON MEDITATION

* Start with five minutes and gradually increase the amount of time. On days when I'm in a hurry and resistant to meditating, I only shoot for five minutes, but most of the time, once I'm in it and feel the warm embrace of silence, I stay longer. The sweet spot for me seems to be 15-20 minutes.

* Instead of thinking about how you're going to cram meditation into your busy schedule, think of it more as taking time to get in touch with the best version of yourself and to connect to your true North.

* Like gratitude and appreciation, frequency is more important than duration. Try to meditate every day, even if it's only for a few minutes.

* Many beginning meditators are told to meditate at the same time and in the same place every day. This is great if your schedule allows. If not, fit it in when and where you can. When my schedule gets hectic, I've meditated plenty of times on a hotel room floor, on a city park bench, or wherever I can find the time and space.

* You can meditate regardless of your religious beliefs. It's essentially a form of mind training and concentration, and not a religious practice, although I personally find it to be quite spiritual.

* I've discovered that days when I don't want to meditate are the days I *most* need to.

ONE OF MY FAVORITE MEDITATIONS

I've been a huge fan of this meditation ever since I first discovered it in the book *Silence* by renowned Zen master and peace activist Thich Nhat Hanh. It's the first meditation he learned once he became an ordained novice monk. It brings about gratitude and mindfulness.

Waking up in the morning I smile.

Twenty four brand-new hours are before me.

I vow to live them deeply

And learn to look at everything around me with the eyes of compassion.

When I practice this meditation I change the word "deeply" to "fully." For some reason, I connect more to the word “fully” and it makes the meditation more impactful for me. Do what works for you.

To practice this meditation, sit in your meditative position, and slowly start to connect with your breath. On your in-breath you’ll say the first line silently to yourself. On the out-breath, the second. The third line is for your next in-breath. The last line is for your out-breath. Continue to repeat the mantra for the time you’ve allocated for this meditation.

As you breathe, let the meaning of the words wash over you. This meditation awakens gratitude and appreciation in me. It makes me realize how incredibly lucky I am to get another 24 hours to live. It also motivates me to create my best life knowing that I’ve been given the gift of another day. Lastly, it reminds me of my commitment to fully and passionately live and to have compassion for all living things.

Give this meditation a try. See what feelings, thoughts and inspiration come up.

~ ~ ~

Daily meditation has made a huge difference in my life. It brings me back to my best self and opens the door for me to be the type of person I want to be in the world. If you want to be happier, have less stress, be more at peace and just generally want an overall better quality of life, try meditation.

It will make a difference.

WITH GRATITUDE

To put creative endeavors out into the world takes a village. Thanks to the following people who helped this project take flight.

Sharon and Greg Maffei, Steven Farmer, Mick Easton, Kim West, Rosalena, Bryan, Giancarlo & Alexis Garrett, Mike Gorman, Marcus Goodwin, Laura Reno, Misty Diaz, Rob & Tyler, Sara Vierra, Dirk Sundman, Iain Grae, Robin, James Gamble, Jay De Leon, BrokenBodies.com, Gabe (Son of Handsome), Mark Sperling, Bill Lehman, Ryan Boudreau, Rachel Kimsey, Matt Weight, Arthur Karmen Matthew Tovmasian, Derek Fujikawa, Andrew Tagatz, Chris Collins, Linh Phan, Alesia Hacker, Rhondie Huron, Mike Edelstein, Randall Orr, Nahir Wold, Dennis Herris, Daniel Medal Sr., Natalie Vyce, Chuck Rockwell, Tony Stubblebine, CEO of Coach.me, Sarina Neer, Mary Cheddie, Susan Clark, Theresa Harker, Matt Moren, David Dean Portelli, Phil Mix.

Made in the USA
San Bernardino, CA
10 March 2018